WHAT PEOPLE ARE SAYING ABOUT

THE HEART OF BUSINESS

"After reading many of today's organizational books, I am excited to find *The Heart of Business*. This thought-provoking book cuts through all the excuses for negative results and allows one to look honestly at ourselves and our organizations. It lays the ground work for rebuilding America's business and industry for long term growth and stability.

"This book is a must for building a corporation. It has presented in a clear and precise manner the importance of a value-based organization. Today, our society is confused by the why and wherefores of 'Values.' Dr. Suryoutomo helps the leaders of today's society understand that success can only come, and be maintained over the long run, through the values of the organization and its value-oriented employees.

"This book will not only change the corporate cultures of many organizations, but the very society we live in. It gives me a greater sense of hope for the future, as it sets a direction which seems grounded in the best parts of mankind and not the worst."

—Robert H. Schumacher, *President*
Schumacher Insurance Associates, Inc.

"As we race toward the year 2000, we've got to change paradigms. A new style of leadership is essential. *The Heart of Business* deftly leads us from an environment featuring imbedded structures and indirect communication channels to a climate that's team-oriented, values-based and creativity-driven. Dr. Suryoutomo not only diagnoses the need, he prescribes specific, concrete action steps to reach values-oriented leadership."

—Roger E. Williams, *Executive Director*
Mount Hermon Association, Inc.

"In his *The Heart of Business*, Dr. Suryoutomo reminds us that prior to the establishment of tactics and strategies, organizations and individuals must come to terms with the issue of value-based leadership. It is a lesson worth learning and remembering."

—Cecil Goodgame, *Vice President & Manager*
Dean Witter Reynolds

"*The Heart of Business* transcends the popular practices and notions of today's market place. Herman Suryoutomo succinctly and brilliantly points out the importance of values and ethics as the centerpiece for us as individuals as well as for our culture."

—Harry Edelstein, *Senior Vice President*
Smith Barney Shearson, Inc.

"It was refreshing to read *The Heart of Business*. The lost values of our country is truly an issue that leaders must recognize and start the change to return to the principles that built this country. As Dr. Suryoutomo points out, rebuilding process began with "us" and ends with future generations."

—Howard W. Brubaker, *Manager & Community Leader*
Morton International, Inc.

"A unique treatise. . . . A provocative challenge to traditional views."

—Robert D. Benya, Esq., *Senior Partner*
Quaresma, Benya, Hall, Connich, O'Hara, & Nixon

"Dr. Suryoutomo brings back the importance of the spiritual aspects of business in *The Heart of Business*. If spiritual aspects were not important, I would assume businesses would now be run by computers. America's great businesses, however, continue to require the values systems incorporated in this book."

—Terry L. Van Der Aa, *President and Chief Executive Officer*
Vancom Transportation, Inc.

THE
HEART
OF
BUSINESS

Rediscovering America's
Ultimate Competitive Weapon
in the Global Marketplace

HERMAN SURYOUTOMO, Ph.D.

All Rights Reserved
Innova Publishing
P.O. Box 3502
Fremont, CA 94539
(510) 745-0200

ISBN: 0-9641179-0-8

Library of Congress Cataloging in Publication Data

Suryoutomo, Ph.D., Herman
    The Heart of Business: Rediscovering America's
    Ultimate Competitive Weapon in the Global Marketplace
    1. Leadership   2. Business Philosophy   3. Corporate
            turnarounds—Management

Includes bibliographical references.

Printed in the United States of America by
Blue Dolphin Press, Inc., Grass Valley, California

HOW TO ORDER:
Quantity discounts are available from the publisher,
INNOVA Publishing, P.O. Box 3502, Fremont, CA 94539;
Telephone (510) 745-0200; FAX (510) 745-7124. On your
letterhead please include information concerning the
intended use of the books and the number of books you
wish to purchase. See last page.

DEDICATION

To my wife, Lucy and
my children, David, Nina, Jason and Tanya,
who give me joy today and optimism for tomorrow.
Whom I love with a passion
that time only strengthens

Table of Contents

Author's Preface

A century ago, Alfred North Whitehead said, "America is great because America is good; and if she ever ceases to be good, she will cease to be great."

This is the core issue of *The Heart of Business*. Our loss of values has cost America our competitive weapon in the global marketplace. That is also the issue that most leadership books evade.

America became a great country because of the values it inspired throughout the world:

- Honesty
- Pride in performance
- A spirit of fair play
- A deep-seated commitment to excellence
- Personal courage
- Credibility
- A sincere concern for others
- Teamwork
- A belief in overcoming obstacles, no matter how challenging

For more than 200 years, America has symbolized quality, dependability, achievement and the soaring spirit of freedom. But somewhere, somehow we have lost sight of the vital connection between our values and our greatness.

We are now scrambling to catch up with a number of powerful countries by trying to adjust to everyone's values, rather than rediscovering the values that made us great.

Today, our corporate leaders talk about treating people better so they will buy into the company's goals, and about the need for excellence, peak performance and zero-defect quality in products. But nobody, it seems, is addressing the critical issue—that this country has slipped in global leadership because our values have been eroded at every level of business and culture.

That slippage now threatens to place our country so far behind international competition that it may be impossible to regain prominence.

The only hope for regaining our international influence is to understand what made us great in the first place and to return to a values-based corporate environment of pride in performance, commitment, personal courage, a genuine concern for others, a strong belief system and integrity.

The strategies in *The Heart of Business* directly address specific challenges that face the nation's millions of leaders every day, whether they make potato chips or microchips, whether they work for small companies or giant multinationals, and whether they have been working in their positions for 20 minutes or 20 years.

It is only as we reawaken, and lead others to reawaken, the values that made America great that we can hope to recapture our competitive edge in the world.

This message has gone largely unsounded in America, so it is especially ironic that a person who spent his first two decades in poverty on the other side of the globe has come to the forefront to proclaim this vital, timely, significant truth. Yet, I have avoided the increasingly popular America-bashing theme and offer practical ideas on how to reach our potential.

Business is going to need an influx of values-based leaders to meet the demands of the future. Simply stated, the purpose of this book is to assist people throughout any organization to discover how to be flexible, creative and effective in self-management and team leadership.

The Heart of Business can be every reader's answer to low morale and productivity, as well as the turbulence and distress already confronting most individuals, corporations, and other organizations. Moreover, it is an urgent call for America's leaders and corpora-tions to move powerfully and confidently into the 21st century.

Introduction

I like the dreams of the future better than the history of the past. [1]

THOMAS JEFFERSON

PERSPECTIVE

This book is written for leaders, managers and employees who are trying to understand the constantly changing values in today's global marketplace.

Since childhood in Indonesia, and through several decades of heading successful businesses in the United States, I have remained firmly in favor of leadership by heartfelt values. I have been dedicated to challenging the idea of a cut-throat or a stab-in-the-back mentality. No one has to look far for the worker alienation, low productivity and leadership burnout which happens when a narcissistic mindset reigns.

Yet I don't believe in "going back to the good old days." Those times exist only in the minds of backward-looking people. Instead, I want to help you to anticipate the coming changes positively. I want to support the view that change can be values-oriented, energizing and creative in today's corporations.

VALUES

Do you share the frustration of so many who attempt to lead fragmented organizations in today's highly competitive business world?

In talking to leaders, both in the United States and abroad, I hear of their frustrations after spending huge sums of money on *systems*—the "latest" quality formula, the "newest" team-building procedure, the "optimum" leadership campaign or the "most effective" customer-service program—only to be disappointed with minimal results.

The story I hear repeatedly is that some people come out of the new programs charged up and ready to apply what they have learned; yet the majority of employees seem to revert to the way they had performed.

What frustrates so many leaders is that the programs *do* cover all the issues that need to be covered. The problem: These systems build on the same old mentality.

There is a solution, and it relates to both values and leadership.

QUESTIONS

What if you could discover a straightforward, insightful way to move your organization away from dissension and selfishness, moving it toward unity and team-oriented success?

How would this benefit your company?

I firmly believe that any organization can move past traditional barriers and ingrained habits to a new, values-based, team-oriented, creativity-fostering way of thinking. That way is *The Heart of Business*.

BACKGROUND DYNAMICS

I have known life from both ends of the continuum. I grew up as an impoverished, lonely child in Indonesia. I almost died from malnutrition and filthy living conditions. Yet I never gave up my dream of coming to the United States. That dream has been fulfilled, and I have been blessed to become an engineer, owner and CEO of numerous businesses and management/educational consultant.

Much of my adult life has been spent helping organizations— from large, nationally-known corporations to smaller, entrepreneurial firms—respond to specific challenges facing most enterprises and employee levels.

I have learned many simple guidelines for achievement in today's complicated world. These principles are the foundations for this book.

WHO SHOULD READ THIS BOOK?

Business is going to need an influx of values-based leaders to meet the demands of the future. Simply stated, my purpose throughout this book is to assist people throughout the entire corporation to discover how to be flexible, creative and effective in self-management and team leadership.

David Campbell, a best-selling author and professor at the Center for Creative Leadership, has written, "Leadership is any ac*tion* that focuses *resources* to create *new opportunities*."

My goal is to help you understand what your values are and to assist you not only in focusing on your strengths, but also in inspiring and motivating others toward shared goals. You will discover new insights in the value of teamwork, and how to be a leader on your team, regardless of your specific role or job description.

This book is for you if . . .

- You have a strong desire to fulfill you leadership potential.

- You have a sincere ambition to be a more effective leader, regardless of your present corporate situation.

- You want to position yourself as a qualified, trustworthy professional who can inspire others to achieve better results, even in the face of challenge, uneasiness and change.

- You want to help create a atmosphere in your organization that fosters creativity, innovation and intuitive opportunities.

If you want your organization to succeed, again and again, during the remainder of the 1990s, and if you desire to create new openings in the marketplace for yourself and your team, this book can make a difference for you.

THE HEART OF BUSINESS — AN OVERVIEW

In PART I — **CHALLENGES OF THE HEART**, you will gain insights into the scope of the problems facing every leader or potential leader throughout each corporation around the world.

In PART II — **READINESS OF THE HEART**, you will discover the foundations of values-based leadership.

PART III — **VISION OF THE HEART**—details specific values-based leadership skills needed by organizations and individuals as we move into the 21st century.

I have included a **VALUES SELF-CHECK** at six strategic places in the book; also, at the end of each chapter, I have placed a summary section entitled **VALUES TO REMEMBER**.

You can turn this book from a passive to an active experience. You alone can make reading these pages a transformational time, not just informational. The key to a values-based life, after all, is personal ownership of values.

VALUES SUMMARY

The Heart of Business has evolved from thousands of hours spent working with some of the most interesting people and corporations, in America and around the globe.

For help, these organizations develop new standards of leadership and organizational excellence. What I have discovered, from individual and collective research, refutes many long-held beliefs and leadership stereotypes. I will use many of these patterns and actual stories throughout the book. [2]

Now, more than ever, I firmly believe that no organization can maintain excellence without an entirely new understanding of values and the ability to implement a shift in attitude.

Leadership must become a process of self-development that can be used by many to bring forth the best from themselves and others.

The Heart of Business can be your answer to the low productivity, turbulence and distress already facing most corporations, organizations and individuals.

Above all, I wish you the best as you begin your journey into a bold, new values-based world.

Herman Suryoutomo, MS, MBA, Ph.D., P.E.

PART I

CHALLENGES OF THE HEART

Chapter 1

VALUES UNDER SIEGE

Chapter 2

THE VALUE OF VALUES

Chapter 3

HOW TO ASSESS YOUR VALUES

ONE

Values Under Siege

I firmly believe that any organization, in order to survive and achieve success, must have a sound set of beliefs. Next, I believe that the most important factor in corporate success is faithful adherence to those beliefs.

TOM WATSON, JR.
Former IBM CEO

FALLEN LEADERS

In 1923, a group of the world's most successful financiers met at a Chicago hotel. Among those present were these nine men:

- The former president of the largest independent steel company in the world.
- The nation's best-known wheat and commodity speculator.
- The president of the New York Stock Exchange.
- The secretary of the interior of President Warren Harding's Cabinet.
- The president of the Bank of International Settlements.
- The man, known as the "Match King," who headed one of the world's prime monopolies.
- The man who was one of the most successful stock speculators on Wall Street.
- A past chairman of the one of the country's largest utility companies.
- The former president of the largest gas company in the United States.

3

Collectively, these tycoons controlled more wealth than existed in the United States Treasury. For years, newspapers and magazines had been printing their success stories. The youth of the nation had been challenged to follow the lofty examples of these six men.

Twenty-five years later, the names remained etched in history, but time had changed everything:

- Charles Schwab, the president of Bethlehem Steel, lived on borrowed money the last five years of his life and died penniless.

- Arthur Cutten, the great wheat speculator, died abroad in poverty.

- Richard Whitney, former president of the New York Stock Exchange, served time in Sing Sing for grand larceny.

- Albert Fall, once a respected member of the president's Cabinet, was pardoned from prison so he could die at home.

- Leon Fraser, president of the Bank of International Settlement,committed suicide.

- Ivar Krueger, the head of the world's greatest monopoly— International Match Corporation—died tragically; whether he was murdered or committed suicide was never established.

- Jesse Livermore, called "the most wondrous of the boy wonders of Wall Street," died by suicide.

- Samuel Insull, once chairman of Commonwealth Edison Company and other utility corporations, was acquitted on embezzlement and mail-fraud charges. He died in Paris in modest surroundings.

- Howard Hopson, the president of the Associated Gas and Electric utility empire, served time in prison for mail fraud, and eventually died in a sanitarium.

All of these men had learned how to make money. All were considered to be top leaders. All were hailed in the press.

We don't have to judge these men or their standards. History has done that for us. Instead, we should learn from their mistakes.

CHALLENGES

We don't have to go back to 1923 to dredge up fallen leaders. The past three decades have brought well-publicized leadership traged-ies: from the highest elected position in the land (John F. Kennedy's "Bay of Pigs," Lyndon B. Johnson's Vietnam, Richard Nixon's Watergate, Jimmy Carter's Iran Hostages, Ronald Reagan's Iran-Contra scandal), to the business world (most notably Ivan Boesky, Michael Milken and Leona Helmsley), and even the religious world (Jim Bakker and Jimmy Swaggart).

In recent Lou Harris polls, public opinion concerning leadership continues to flounder. Of the adults questioned, 55% expressed feel-ings of estrangement from leadership. Confidence in the United States Supreme Court has dropped from a high of 58% in 1966 to 28%. During the same time frame, faith in the press has fallen from 38% to 18%, in college presidents from 58% to 34%, and in Wall Street leaders from 26% to only 10%.

Similar declines in corporate confidence leave only 18% of those polled feeling that they can count on business leaders, while only 14% express trust in labor union leaders.

This situation is bound to get worse before it gets better. There is only one solution: building a values-based foundation today for tomorrow's leaders.

LEADERSHIP OPPORTUNITIES

The heart of successful business doesn't lie in the fast deal and the quick buck. It isn't kept in bank vaults and it isn't represented by high-grade securities. It lies in values-based, creative, innovative, team-oriented leadership.

This firm conviction is the foundation of *The Heart of Business*, and essential to every strategy that I present throughout this book.

I believe the need for values-based, across-the-board leadership will loom larger as organizations move into the 21st century. Here are six reasons that values-based leadership must be fostered through all levels of corporations:

(1) *Established corporate rules are constantly evolving.*

Leaders can no longer force values upon their people. Strategies that worked yesterday—in any area of business—may continue to work for you tomorrow, or they may work against you.

(2) *Businesses and individuals are in turmoil today.*

As I work with organizations of all sizes and marketplace niches, I never cease to be amazed at the widespread absence of values, mission and understanding. I find instead disillusionment, stress, burnout, turnover, inefficiency, indecision, stagnation and evidences of "right person/wrong place."

(3) *Mechanistic management procedures are increasingly ineffective.*

Heavy-handed, boss-versus-subordinate boundaries will continue to be demonstrated in non-visionary companies, but these outdated methods will also continue to cause worker alienation and leader disillusionment.

(4) *The trend toward decentralization in government is paralleled in corporate management.*

The pace is already being set by new entrepreneurial and intrapreneurial firms that have sprung up across the nation and world. Organizations that do not develop a strong set of values simply will not survive.

(5) *Values-based, trend-setting leaders will surround themselves with like-minded people.*

Pioneers are discovering the need for a focus on values, excellence, energetic innovation and customer-oriented service, not dull sameness and mindless hierarchy.

(6) *Employees will be unwilling to work for organizations that are unwilling to build people through values, shared opportunity, identity, responsibility and ownership.*

Tomorrow's innovators will no longer do tasks by rote. As human-resource assets shrink, employees will be able to demand more from organizations. Work will become less of a controlling factor in life. Values will play an increasing role.

Too many organizations are content with yesterday's solutions. That is sad (and costly), because today's problems need visionary leaders.

Leadership is not the exclusive domain of a gifted few, but is a process of self-development that can be used by many to bring forth the best from themselves and others. The stronger your set of values, the more permanent your success becomes. Tomorrow's corporations will require an entirely new breed of people who understand and model this kind of values-based, dynamic, innovative leadership.

Why?

CHANGES

Leadership is being transformed. According to John Naisbitt, author of **Megatrends**, during the coming years, leadership will be marked by a spreading move toward decentralization, and decisions will be increasingly made at the lowest possible level. As a result, leadership will be transformed into completely new patterns. Without broad-based, deeply-sown values, no corporation can thrive for long.

The work force is being revolutionized. The predominantly white-male work force is rapidly becoming a memory. By the year 2000, 80% of women between the ages of 25 and 54 will head for the work place each morning, compared with 70% today. Minorities will account for a quarter of the labor force, up from one-fifth. [1]

The market place is being refashioned. During the past 10 years, American business has experienced the most turbulent time in history. A glance at the front page of any Wall Street Journal or Barron's gives ample evidence of market-place turbulence: bankruptcies, fragile markets, cultural gyrations, apprehension, downsizings and mergers.

Companies are in a quickening state of flux. Currently 30%, or 3.5 million, of all U.S. businesses are owned by women. By 2000, that figure should be 50%. At the same time, of the top 100 companies on the original Fortune 500 list in 1955, only 46 remain in the top 100 today. If anything, those drop-out figures have speeded-up during the past decade. Mergers and acquisitions have played a part in these changes. Changes in corporate structures have been unpredictable, at best.

The international economy is evolving quickly. Europe is becoming an economic superpower. With 320 million prospering consumers, it is now the world's richest market. This striking revival resulted from the elimination of nearly 300 separate trade barriers among the dozen once-squabbling nations of the European Economic Community. How is Japan faring? At present, Japanese investors are borrowing money against their Tokyo land holdings and using the loans to invest in U.S. real estate. Hypothetically, by using the real-estate value of Tokyo as collateral, Japanese investors could borrow $7.7 trillion and buy all the land in the U.S., all the companies in the New York Stock Exchange, NASDAQ, and several other exchanges—and still get $1.4 trillion in change. An article in *U.S. World & News Report* summarized the international turbulence:

> *Nobody ever claimed it was easy, but winning in the global market place is about to get even harder. Not because the world economy will fizzle (growth promises to be buoyant), or because U.S. industry has grown flabby (it's in far better shape than in 1980). Rather, competition is evolving from merely brutal to downright bone-crushing. GE Chairman Jack Welch has already dubbed the '90s "the white knuckle decade." Perhaps 'bare knuckle' better sums up the situation.* [2]

Change itself is in a major transition. Two decades ago, noted futurist Alvin Toffler made this startling statement:

> *Change is avalanching upon our heads and most people are grotesquely unprepared to cope with it. . . . For what is occurring now is, in all likelihood, bigger, deeper, and more important than the industrial revolution. Indeed, a growing body of reputable opinion asserts that the present movement represents nothing less than the second great divide in human history, comparable in magnitude only with that first great break in historic continuity, the shift from barbarism to civilization.* [3]

More specifically, according to Toffler, these changes will happen at an accelerated rate:

> *This lifetime is also different from all others because of the astonishing expansion of the scale and scope of change. . . . We have not merely extended the scope and scale of change, we have radically altered its pace. We have in our time released a totally new social force—a stream of change so accelerated that it influences our sense of time, revolu-*

tionizes the tempo of daily life, and affects the very way we "feel" the world around us. [4]

Time has proved that Toffler's predictions were hardly a collection of simulated, book-selling gimmicks. Other business-oriented futurists, including Tom Peters, Marilyn Ferguson, Peter Drucker and John Naisbitt, have since pointed to even more specific trends which will revolutionize most of our established foundations.

CHANGE DYNAMICS

Much of my adult life has been spent building organizations of varying sizes—from real-estate development to real-estate brokerage; from engineering to management consulting; from computer assembly to software development, and from fast-food restaurant development to construction. I know what it is like to feel responsible for hundreds of people's lives. Leadership, believe me, is not for wimps.

Based on trends I see on the horizon, I believe that during the coming decade the business environment will be more unpredictable than ever—more so than most industry analysts are forecasting.

Corporations with no firm values that continue to use outdated methods simply will not outlast the turbulence, and neither will the people within them. Financial, technological and marketplace changes will come fast and furiously, and only the strongest, most flexible organizations—those that can learn to live with the turmoil—will survive.

Yet, during the coming chaos, there will also be a growing number of people and corporations who will flourish, despite the obstacles.

How? By practicing the *Heart of Business.*

TERMS

Some interesting terms have entered the corporate vocabulary. "Excellence," "megatrends," "high-tech," "high-touch," "service imperative"—to name a few.

"Value" is an old word with new meaning for today's leaders. It comes from a French/Latin root that is tied to worth. Simply stated, value means "to think highly of; to prize."

Values—the most highly-prized and esteemed of all characteris-

9

tics—are the greatest needs, today and tomorrow, among leaders. A values-based mindset includes a combination of beliefs, trust, strategic thinking, teamwork, quality, customer service, policy implementation and an inspirational corporate culture.

The Heart of Business expresses and designates the flexible, participative corporate system that will dominate tomorrow's marketplace. It is a high-touch, high-service, multipurpose approach to leadership, customer-orientation and work relationships.

I firmly believe that it is imperative that specific values-based traits be adopted across the board, not just among those in traditional "leadership" or managerial functions. This call for putting the heart into business will be the foremost differentiating factor between tomorrow's champions (on a corporate and personal scale) and could-have-beens. Too much in today's world is changing for outdated thinking to endure.

CHALLENGES

It should be apparent that the obstacles facing organizations today demand fundamentally new modes of thinking and acting. Only those courageous corporations and organizations that successfully tackle today's problems with tomorrow's solutions will have the leadership capabilities to deal with change.

Like it or not, corporations are already locked into critical confrontations and difficulties. As mentioned earlier, change is taking place at an accelerating rate. This should not be a frightening time, but it should be a season of questions and new directions. Lee Iacocca often quips, "There is nothing better than a life-and-death struggle to help get your priorities straight."

John Sculley, former CEO of the Apple Corporation, wrote:

> . . . When most companies are confronted with problems, they try simply to fix them. They fail to use a problem or a crisis as an opportunity to explore a new way to do business. Managers' first instinct is to fix instead of revel, to solve a problem instead of find an opportunity. Before they ask, "how do I make it beautiful or better," they ask, "how do I get out of this jam?" It's far more important to get interested in taking a problem or crisis apart and understanding it.[5]

The purpose of this book is to help you become a leader who is ready to create, not one who is merely content to fix. Therefore, as you read, keep an open mind. Remember John Stuart Mill's words:

No great improvements in the lot of mankind are possible, until a great change takes place in the fundamental constitution of their modes of thought.

Thankfully, there exist a growing number of organizations (and individuals within those enterprises) engaged in courageous leadership explorations of beliefs and values. These trail-blazers are committed to making a difference, both in organizational output and human enjoyment. These leadership champions want all employees to view themselves as essential people in the personal and professional pursuit of quality life.

You can join this ongoing experiment.

VALUES SUMMARY

In the midst of change, how do you ensure your company's survival and success? It is a question that I have been asked hundreds of times.

I have but one answer: Practice the *Heart of Business*. Only the most creative, adaptable, participative corporate system will be able to build stable, long-term empowerment, growth and productivity.

Wrote David Schwartz, Ph.D., author of the best-selling book, *The Magic of Thinking Big*:

Persons who reach the top rungs in business management, selling, engineering, religious work, writing, acting, and in every other pursuit get there by following conscientiously and continuously a plan for self-development and growth.

I believe that values-based leadership will never again be monopolized by a few; instead this avenue will be opened to men and women from all levels of the work force. Values-based leadership must become a process of self-development which can be used by many to bring forth the best from themselves and others.

The Heart of Business: It can be your answer to the turbulence that faces corporations, organizations and individuals.

Values to Remember

(1) We can learn from the mistakes of leaders who learned how to make money and attract power, but who never learned how to live.

(2) Leadership, more than ever, is one of the most challenged institutions in our society.

(3) Every person in your organization must become a values-based, creative, innovative, team-oriented leader.

(4) Changes are happening at an accelerated rate.

(5) Values—the most highly-prized and esteemed of all characteristics—are the greatest needs, today and tomorrow, among leaders.

(6) *The Heart of Business* expresses and designates the flexible, participative corporate system that will dominate tomorrow's marketplace.

We have come to worship production as an end in itself, which of course it is not. It is precisely there that the honest critic of our way of life makes his attack and finds us vulnerable. Sure there must be for each person some ultimate value, some purpose, some mode of self-expression that makes the experience we call life richer and deeper. [6]

CLARENCE B. RANDALL
Former President of Inland Steel

TWO

The Value of Values

To be persuasive, we must be believable; to be believable, we must be credible; to be credible, we must be truthful.

EDWARD R. MURROW
Pioneer Broadcaster

LASTING EXAMPLES

Jack Griffin wrote an essay many years ago that has since become a classic. It still bears reading:

When Johnny was 6 years old, he was with his father when they were caught speeding. His father handed the officer a $20 bill with his driver's license. "It's OK, son," his father said as they drove off. "Everybody does it."

When he was 8, he was present at a family council presided over by Uncle George, on the surest means to shave points off the income-tax return. "It's OK, kid," his uncle said. "Everybody does it."

When he was 9, his mother took him to his first theater production. The box office man couldn't find any seats until his mother discovered an extra $5 in her purse. "It's OK, son," she said. "Everybody does it."

When he was 12, he broke his glasses on the way to school. His Aunt Francine persuaded the insurance company that they had been stolen and they collected $75. "It's OK, kid," she said. "Everybody does it."

When he was 15, he made right guard on the high-school football team. His coach showed him how to block and at the same time grab the opposing end by the shirt so the official couldn't see it. "It's OK, kid," the coach said. "Everybody does it."

When he was 16, he took his first summer job at the supermarket. His assignment was to put the over-ripe strawberries in the bottom of the boxes and the good ones on top where they would show. "It's OK, kid," the manager said. "Everybody does it."

When he was 18, Johnny and a neighbor applied for a college scholarship. Johnny was a marginal student. His neighbor was in the upper 3 percent of his class, but he couldn't play right guard. Johnny got the scholarship. "It's OK, son," his parents said. "Everybody does it."

When he was 19, he was approached by an upperclassman who offered the test answers for $50. "It's OK, kid," he said. "Everybody does it."

Johnny was caught and sent home in disgrace. "How could you do this to your mother and me?" His father said. "You never learned anything like this at home." His aunt and uncle were also shocked.

"If there's one thing the adult world can't stand, it's a kid who cheats!" [1]

What does a story like that have to do with business survival and success?

Everything!

ACHIEVERS

Values-based leaders can inspire higher standards of excellence in corporations and organizations. In every walk of life, the focus on values must be on results: satisfied customers, fulfilled team-members, and profitable companies. In a complacent corporate world that is too often willing to put up with shoddiness, the rewards have never been greater—in terms of pay, privilege, power and perks—

for values-oriented leaders who consistently and creatively perform.

Three special qualities common to results-oriented leaders are:

(1) *Hard work*

For those whose hearts are in their business, a difficult task as a challenge and source of enjoyment. If your job leaves you bored and frustrated, look for a way to use your experience and skills in a field that will give you more satisfaction. The odds are the change will also translate into improved performance and success.

(2) *Goal setting*

Set realistic short-, mid- and long-range goals that are high enough to be a challenge. Start small and build on each success. The goals should encompass every area of life.

(3) *A desire to learn*

Keep in mind that, in the information age, continuing education is increasingly important to success. But be forewarned: while a desire to learn is a prerequisite for leadership, a degree is hardly a guarantee of success. There is a major difference between education and learning.

Hard work, goal setting and a desire to learn are qualities every leader can cultivate.

I learned these facts of life during my childhood, but perhaps my greatest test was after I came to America on a Fulbright Scholarship to attend graduate school.

For me, hard work and persistence was the only way to escape poverty and death was to become a successful person. These qualities were more than survival, however, since they were the only way I could ever make a difference for myself and others in life.

I arrived in America wearing flimsy Indonesian shoes, hardly appropriate for winter in the Midwest, After the first few snows, my shoes cracked and leaked moisture.

I had no jacket and wore tropical, light shirts. This was fine during the early fall, but when the temperature began dropping down to 10 degrees, the only way I could keep warm was to run from my tiny dormitory room to classrooms, stopping in front of buildings to warm myself, then running again to my destination.

I must have been quite a sight to others. It was often very cold, windy and stormy, and I would arrive at classes with my teeth chattering and my face feeling frozen. It was so cold.

On top of that, there were many additional problems. My master's degree from Indonesia was not recognized by the college in America, so during the first year I had to retake 22 course units by examination. All of this was in addition to taking my regular course load, doing research, and working at a job to pay for my dorm room and enough food to eat. To maintain my partial scholarship, I had to maintain an "A" average and to be at the top of my class because there was such heavy competition for the scholarship.

I had borrowed money to come to America, and I knew that if I failed in school, I would have to return to Indonesia and work for much of the rest of my life to pay off my debt.

I got very discouraged during that first winter, and I sometimes wondered, "Should I just give up? Should I just return home?"

One day, I was very tired so I went down to the laundry to wash my clothing. It was late at night and it was frigid and blowing snow outside.

To most American students at the time, perhaps, washers and dryers were commonplace. For me, they were a source of awe. We certainly had not had a dryer in the shanty where I grew up, since we washed clothes in the water and dried them in the sun.

I brought books with me to the laundry room, but on this particular occasion I started noticing how the clothes went up and down, up and down in the dryer. I kept watching, and it was fascinating to me. I began realizing that there, in a very simple picture, was a snapshot of what life was like. Seeing the clothes tumbling up and down, I suddenly caught a revelation of how life was a series of cycles.

If I could survive the down time, next it would be up. Sure more down times would come, but more up times would come, too.

I realize that this was, perhaps, no great revelation to someone else, but it was exactly the picture I need to remind me of a very important concept. It bolstered me at a very low point in my life. Suddenly I felt buoyant again. I became more determined than ever

—to make something of myself in America—to never, ever give up. No matter how much I had to work and learn in order to be the top student, I would make that sacrifice.

I had to take charge of my life, even if I were down. That attitude helped me accept the reality that as a foreign student, I had to work harder than most young people to overcome my handicaps of language.

Time flew. My 22 credits by examination were approved. The cold winter turned into spring. I went on to pass with honors and eventually I received my Master's Degree (and later my doctorate). Once I held my American diploma in my hand and was offered a good job, I felt, for the first time, that I would be able to stay in here and to realize my dream to make a difference in other people's life.

For me, you or anyone, leadership must be built on hard work, goal setting and a desire to learn. But that is just the beginning.

Values-based leadership, must go much deeper, for it must be built on deeply-held beliefs.

LEADERSHIP WITHIN

Leadership begins deep inside you. It starts with your values— the characteristics you esteem most highly.

I have spent most of my lifetime studying to learn what makes leaders reach the top. Here, I feel, are the eight major values needed to help you become a person who can be an "inner winner":

(1) *Honesty*

Nearly every major survey of leaders has one characteristic that is placed, invariably, at the top of the list. That valuable trait is *honesty*, which means to be held in respect, free from deceit.

James Kouzes and Barry Posner, in conjunction with professor Warren Schmidt, the American Management Association and the Federal Executive Institute Alumni Association, surveyed thousands of workers. They asked them what they considered to be the most important leadership traits. Eighty-three percent of them expressed belief that people must be honest before workers will call them leaders. [2]

Yet according to a recent New York Times/CBS poll of workers, only 32% of the public believes that most corporate executives are honest. Conversely, 55% think that most are not honest! There is clearly a gap between what we admire and what the public thinks it is getting.

As a values-based leader, you must be honest. It is the very least that your people deserve. Teamwork will never develop until people trust in your leadership character, and it all begins with honesty.

A CASE IN WHICH HONESTY PAID OFF

Basic honesty paid off for David, a salesman in his early 30s who came to me looking for a job during a crisis in his personal life.

David had been a salesman for a food company, and had been financially successful. He had a big house in the suburbs, two cars, a boat and many other accessories to the good life. But after 10 years of marriage and three sons, he and his wife couldn't stand the sight of each other.

To cap it all, David lost his job.

A week after the layoff, he and his wife were quarreling over breakfast, and she shouted the fateful words: "I want a divorce." And she kicked him out of the house.

David saw my company's sign as he drove past. He stopped and told the receptionist he wanted to see the president. She directed him to me.

"I need a job, and I will do anything," he told me after the introductions.

David didn't try to feed me a line. He told me that he lived in a very nice area and had three fine children, but was in deep trouble.

"I'm in the process of getting a divorce," he said, "and it pains me to think about it. I love my wife and children and I want to hold them together. What I need is advice on how to get along with my wife, and I need a job badly."

I didn't need a salesman, at least not one with David's sales background. But something about his candor, honesty and fresh approach appealed to me. He could have given me all kinds of reasons for leaving his previous job and wanting to come to work for me. But he was open and honest.

I told him to give me a call later and we'd talk some more about his problems.

He called several days later and we met again. I decided to offer him a temporary position. It was work that had to be done, and he had the skills for it.

Because of the circumstances of our meeting, I took a special interest in David. He was warm, open-minded and teachable.

At first, his wife was skeptical about his new attitude. She thought it was just a ploy to keep her from going through with the divorce. But as months went by, she saw a real change in his life. Later, David found a great job in his field in another city. It was close to their parents and other relatives. I encouraged him to take the job.

As I think back, it was David's honesty and little else that got him the job with me. A week earlier I had interviewed a much more likely prospect for the job. He had come into my office brimming with confidence, and the interview went great. It was obvious that he had a good background and knew our field well. He had just quit a high-level position with a competitor of ours after four years with that company.

I was about to hire him when he played what he must have thought was his trump card. He possessed confidential information about his former employer that would give us an edge in competition. He promised me that if I hired him I would get all the information I needed.

My admiration for him turned to disrespect. My principles place honesty, integrity and ethics above short-term gain. If he would sell out his former employer, he wouldn't hesitate to sell me out if we ever parted ways.

Stealing each other's secrets may be a common practice among the high-tech companies surrounding me in Silicon Valley, but I wanted no part of it. I wanted no part of anyone who practiced that kind of business ethics. David might have been less qualified as a salesperson in our field, but I felt I could trust him, so he got the job.

The rewards for being honest are immeasurable. They come not just in the form of immediate benefits, but also in sustained leadership and long-range productivity. It isn't measured by degrees. You either have it or you don't.

(2) *Integrity*

This trait, which is defined as having sound moral principles, goes beyond honesty. Honesty suggests being free of deceit. Integrity suggests doing what is right, no matter what. Though neither trait is passive, integrity seems to be the most active of the two.

Consistency between word and deed is one of the principal criteria by which people judge your integrity. This characteristic is the companion to honesty and is an absolute necessity if you are to build a career working with people.

A friend of mine—we'll call him George—had a lucrative sales position with a large manufacturing company. His territory took in the entire state. Although he loved selling, the travel was hard on him and his family. But something else bothered him about the job. The company's management had absolutely no respect for its employees. Among other indignities, salespeople had to make hourly calls to their district managers detailing everything they had done except going to the john.

One Sunday afternoon, George took a call from the national vice president in charge of sales. The executive said George's district manager was being moved to the main office and George had been chosen to succeed him. He would get a substantial raise, a company car and an expense account, as well as other perks.

That was the good news.

The bad news was that the vice president wanted to get together with George to go over all the reports. George would have to monitor the sales reps he was supervising, identify their problems, determine what kind of mess they were in and keep them in line.

As they spoke, George began to realize how unhappy he had been in this autocratic environment.

After he had hung up, his wife noticed the gloom on his face.

"What's the matter, hon? Did you get laid off or fired?"

"Worse than that," replied George. "They want me to become one of them."

George thought about his options. He needed the job. Although he had a healthy income, he also had an expensive lifestyle, and he was actually just a few months away from bankruptcy. If he lost his job, he would be in serious trouble. But if he accepted the promotion, he would be unable to look himself in the eye.

George called the national sales executive back and told him he had decided to resign from the company. Then he told his wife to call a baby sitter. They were going away for the weekend to renew their commitment to their marriage and to celebrate his liberation from an oppressive employer.

I'm happy to say that George later became the successful head of a large sales organization.

As George told me about his decision, I thought about an earlier decision of my own. Early in my career, I held a key position with a professional organization, which I helped develop from a five-person operation to one with more than 500 professionals.

I was excited about the company because it embodied many of the ideals that I embrace. It practiced honesty and integrity and it was people-oriented; yet it also provided a lucrative income.

Soon we began to bring in top-level people from other large organizations. Suddenly, instead of working hard for the common goal of serving our customers, these people began to jockey for power. They began to look out for their pocketbooks instead of guarding the interests of the company, its employees and customers.

In time, the company adopted a policy of maximizing profits, sometimes at all costs and seemingly without regard for the interests of our customers and employees.

Finally, I decided to leave and start my own company. I had spent considerable time watching that company grow, but I couldn't stay with it at the expense of my integrity.

(3) Character/credibility

Character—who you really are—is reflected in your "credit rating" with people around you. Your character determines your credibility. People who build reputations for excellent character will hold the respect and loyalty of those with whom they work.

Leadership analysts James Kouzes and Barry Posner:

> Credibility is one of the hardest attributes to earn. And it is the most fragile of human qualities. It is earned minute by minute, hour by hour, month by month, year by year. But it can be lost in very short order if not attended to. We are willing to forgive a few minor transgressions, a slip of the tongue, a misspoken word, a careless act. But there comes a time when enough is enough. And when leaders have used up all their credibility, they will find that it is nearly impossible to earn it back. [3]

Character is the essence of leadership.

(4) *Courage*

My first lesson in courage came from my mother.

My parents were once quite wealthy in Indonesia, but I was born too late to enjoy it. They lost everything during World War II. Instead of great wealth, I inherited poverty.

My father died when I was six, and when I was eight my mother, then 54, suffered from acute leukemia. She was in and out of a coma, with blood seeming to ooze from every pore of her body. But she knew that if she died I would be left alone in poverty. So she fought her illness with great courage and determination. Through some kind of miracle, she survived.

Her valor provided the example that sustained me through a similar trial. When I was in senior high school, I was hospitalized and bedridden for a year as a result of malnutrition and other illnesses resulting from childhood poverty. Our shanty was next to a sewer that overflowed with human wastes. I shared a room with dozens of rats, hundreds of cockroaches and untold thousands of termites. No wonder my health gave out.

As things got worse, my morale hit bottom. I was full of pain and I couldn't move. I began toying with the idea of suicide.

In the depth of my despair, I thought I heard a soothing voice saying, "God be with you. Trust Him. Life is worth living. You are here for a purpose; you can make a difference."

I gathered the courage to live. With a renewed respect for the sanctity of life, I calmed down and began reading an inspirational book. Then I started to dream. In my dreams, I overcame my illness, got up and walked, came to America, became successful, and made a difference in this world.

My dreams came true.

It wasn't easy to follow the dream. My friends thought I was crazy. We knew that it cost almost $10,000 per year for college in America, in addition to living expenses and plane fare. The exchange rate at the time was at least 1,000 Indonesian rupiahs per U.S. dollar. This meant that I would need at least 10 million rupiahs. I had only 15 rupiahs in my pocket and owed the hospital a great deal of money. But I had the courage to dream, and that's what brought me to America.

THE COURAGE TO WALK OUT

In America, I found other examples of courage. Steve and Chris Cummings come immediately to mind.

Steve grew up in a small town, son of a hard-working farmer. He went to college on a track scholarship and student loans. But he injured his foot playing football, and had to undergo surgery requiring 23 incisions.

Later, he married his sweetheart, whom he had known since he was 10, and returned to college. This time, he had to walk a mile to school on crutches and work to pay for his expenses.

After graduating, he quickly climbed the corporate ladder and eventually became corporate accountant for a large wood-product company. He would spend six months writing a $625 million annual budget and six more months implementing it. All expenditures had to pass through him. It was an awesome responsibility for a 27-year-old man.

Steve had an office on the 23rd floor of the Embarcadero Center overlooking San Francisco Bay. He dreamed of becoming a vice president in the company.

Then, when their first son was 5 years old, Chris became pregnant again. One day in late November, she called to tell him something was wrong. She was in pain and she needed him to come home.

As he walked out of the office, his boss came in. The boss had a reputation for unreasonableness.

"Where are you going?" he asked.

"I've got to go home. My wife's having a problem with her pregnancy."

"Oh no you're not. You have a report to do, and you'd better do it before you go home."

Steve had gone deeply in debt to sustain an affluent life style in San Francisco. He needed the job badly. So he stayed and finished the report.

When he got home, he found Chris passed out on the bathroom floor. He rushed her to the hospital to find that she had lost 30% of her blood. People have died after losing only 20%.

Burdened with guilt, Steve made a promise that he would never be in that position again. He would become financially independent so that he could say no to unethical conduct and unreasonable requests.

He left his job and started his own business. He now is a highly successful businessman, because he had the courage to face reality, dream bold dreams and leave a secure job to challenge the unknown.

Courage is defined as the attitude of facing and dealing with anything recognized as dangerous, difficult or painful. It measures your leadership abilities at critical times in life, and it can be developed only in the stress and strain of everyday activities.

SEVEN QUALITIES OF GREAT LEADERS

After years of studying and practicing the techniques of success, I have identified seven qualities that characterize the greatest leaders I have known:

- A proven capability to conceive and implement positive changes.

- A record of keeping commitments, no matter what.

- A capacity for having impact on the opinions and actions of others—an influence so subtle it sometimes goes unrecognized.

- A proficiency at expressing views and perspectives in innovative ways;

- A proficiency at expressing views and perspectives

- An ability to recognize and admit personal mistakes, and to learn from those failures;

- An insight into the nature of organizational structure and political inner workings of the corporation.

- An ability to make things happen.

Without courage, you will never be a values-based leader.

(5) *Tact*

Tact, the delicate perception of the right thing to say or do without offending, implies that you are sensitive to the needs and feelings of others. A values-based leader must know what to say and how to say it with power and persuasion.

Tact is the key ingredient for win/win strategies. We applied it successfully once when I was consulting for a friend who headed a manufacturing company. An inventor had brought suit against the company, claiming that it had stolen one of his ideas.

When I learned about the case, the litigation was already two years old. The inventor was a man in his 40s. He had never finished high school, but had taken electronics courses while in military service, and had studied a great deal on his own. He was convinced that he was right, and he had succeeded in preventing my client from getting the case dismissed.

I looked into the matter and became firmly convinced that my client was morally and legally right. He had not infringed on the inventor's patent. His company had independently developed a device that did roughly the same thing the inventor's device did. But my friend's device was technically more advanced, and it operated through a different mechanism.

My friend and I concluded, though, that it would be futile to try to force the plaintiff to give up. We decided to look for a mutually agreeable solution.

We asked our adversary to dinner. We steered the conversation away from the controversy itself and toward the inventor's motivations. What made him tick?

We discovered that here was a man who was not interested in money and not interested in bringing a large company to its knees. He was the oldest of five children in a poor family and now had four children of his own. He ran his own repair shop and spent most of his evenings working on his inventions. What he really wanted at this point was for someone to respect his intelligence. He loved his work and wanted to be able to do it and receive reasonable compensation for it.

We explained to him why we felt we were entitled to use the invention. But we also acknowledged that he was a brilliant person—the sort of person we'd like to have working for us.

That was exactly what he wanted to hear. We arranged for him to meet with the director of research and development for the company. The company got a brilliant person whose talents it could put to profitable use. The inventor got a good job where he could earn respect and a good salary.

Tact made the difference.

Tact and courage work hand in hand, even though they might seem like opposites. Abraham Lincoln, asked to give his definition of tact, mused, "Well, I guess you might say that it's the knack of letting the other fellow have your way."

Tact means having the savvy to make a point without making an enemy.

(6) *Creativity*

Clear and creative thinking also helps with another must for success: the ability to make decisions. Decision-making is part of a leader's job, and it is a task in which practice takes you closer to perfection.

Analytical thinking, however, cannot overpower creative thinking. Values-based leaders must understand the merit of thinking, of taking time out from the rush of daily life to ponder their work and their goals and to develop "a better way."

That passion for discovering a better way to do something—the product of creative thinking—is what makes achievers stand out from the crowd and move up the ladder.

(7) *Intuition*

One step beyond creativity is intuition. Intuition is defined by Webster's as "the art or faculty of knowing directly, without the use of rational processes."

Most of us have intuitive flashes: We like someone immediately, we're suspicious of someone else without knowing why, or an inner voice tells us that one decision is better than another. We call it a "gut feeling" or "just an inner voice." We should listen more to these feelings.

In the past, rational thinkers have called these on-target intuitions "lucky guesses" or flukes. Increasingly, however, intuition is finding respect, particularly among people in corporate boardrooms.

All business executives who value people's deepest desires should value the tool of intuition.

(8) *Enthusiasm*

Values-based leaders are expected to be enthusiastic, energetic and positive about the future. Leaders are also expected to be inspiring.

This is indeed a characteristic that all champions possess. Mediocre workers could revolutionize their lives with just a dose of enthusiasm. It is undoubtedly one of the great attributes needed to be a leader. It is said that nothing great was ever achieved without enthusiasm. Your enthusiasm projects more about your sincere belief in your leadership abilities than any other single characteristic.

Write the authors of the best-selling book, *The Leadership Challenge*:

> *Not everyone agrees with [the need for enthusiasm]. Some react with discomfort to the idea that being inspiring is an essential leadership quality. One chief executive officer of a large corporation even told us, "I don't trust people who are inspiring." No doubt this is a response to past crusaders who led their followers to death or destruction. Other executives are skeptical of their ability to inspire others. Both are making a terrible mistake. In the final analysis, it is essential that leaders inspire our confidence in the validity of the goal. Enthusiasm and excitement signal the leader's personal commitment to pursuing that dream. If a leader displays no passion for a cause, why should others?* [4]

Why indeed? Enthusiasm is what separated Gerry from the pack when a friend and client of mine was looking around for a successor as CEO of his medium-sized company.

About four years before he embarked on his succession planning, he had hired Gerry, who was only 27 at the time. A good accountant, Gerry knew very little about the manufacturing business. He was hired to take over the administrative and office routine.

But he showed enthusiasm in everything he did. His interest ranged far beyond the narrow bounds of his official duties. Whenever he saw ways to help people in sales or manufacturing, he was there to help. He made a major contribution to the company shortly after joining it. The company didn't have a good benefits program, and as a result it was losing employees to competitors. Gerry came up with a good benefits program, which eventually reduced turnover costs and saved the company money. He studied production and developed cost-benefit ratios for investment in new machinery. This enabled the company to invest wisely and resulted in large cost savings. When the company experienced a sales slump, he looked for ways to boost sales, even though sales was not his area of expertise.

Gerry's enthusiasm paid off not only for the company but for Gerry personally. When we looked over the record, we concluded that he was the logical one to succeed my client and friend as CEO.

VALUES SUMMARY

Are you honest? Are you filled with integrity? Do you have character and credibility? Are you courageous? How about tactful? Creative? Intuitive? Enthusiastic?

Do you have the most needed leadership attributes? Inner leadership begins with the most basic of human attributes. If you accept the challenge of values-based leadership, you put yourself into an exclusive category of people who are willing to make extra sacrifices, to go the extra mile and to find a way to keep themselves as well as their companies' employees, investors and customers satisfied.

That challenge, however, must go much deeper. In Chapter 3, you will be able to assess your values. On that foundation, you can then begin to determine what values you most desire. That action, by itself, puts you head-and-shoulders above most corporate leaders.

Values to Remember

(1) Values-based leaders will be the new celebrities in corporations and organizations.

(2) Hard work, goal setting and a desire to learn—these are qualities every leader can cultivate. But these traits are only beginning points. Values go much deeper.

(3) Leadership begins deep inside you. It starts with your values— the characteristics which you esteem most highly.

(4) Are you honest? Are you filled with integrity? Do you have character and credibility? Are you courageous? How about tactful? Creative? Intuitive? Enthusiastic? These are the values most desired by great leaders.

You can't expect an empty bag to stand up straight. [5]

KENNETH BLANCHARD
and NORMAN VINCENT PEALE

THREE

How to
Assess Your Values

*Surrendering to change means seeing ourselves
differently. A failure to understand the nature of change
is crippling to many of the world's billions.* [1]

DUDLEY LYNCH and PAUL L. KORDIS
Authors and futurists

SELF-PROPHECY

In Bandung, Indonesia, where I used to live, the story is told of
a detective, Mr. Sosrowinarso, who followed another man all over
town. Finally, Sosrowinarso lost sight of the person he was tailing,
but suspected that he had ducked into a certain hotel.

To avoid any suspicion, the detective decided to go into the hotel,
walk up to the desk clerk and ask whether a Mr. Sosrowinarso was
registered there. His plan was to peek quickly at the register while the
clerk was looking for his name on the list. That way he could see
whether the man he was chasing was actually registered at the hotel.

Imagine his surprise when the clerk replied, "Yes, he is registered here. In fact, he is waiting for you in Room Number 10."

Sosrowinarso was stunned. His mind raced: "How did the clerk
know?" He had to follow up this lead, however enigmatic it might be,
so he shrugged his head and headed for Room 10. He hesitated before
knocking, and when he rapped on the door, it slowly opened by
itself.

The man he had been following was himself, only 20 years older.
For a few brief moments, the two Sosrowinarsos talked, and the

conversation altered his life, for it answered all the "If-I-knew-then-what-I-know-now" speculation. He learned what he had to do to be the person he wanted to become—the choices he had to make.

It is only a story, but for each of us there is a person standing just beyond an imaginary door—five years, 10 years, 20 years in the future.

What will you be doing then? Will you be successful and happy? Will you be satisfied with your life?

For the most part, the answers are already staring you in the face. What are you doing now? Are you successful and happy now? Are you satisfied with your life now?

VALUES

Writes Thomas J. Peters and Robert H. Waterman in their classic book, ***In Search of Excellence***:

> *Let us suppose that we were asked for one all-purpose bit of advice for management, one truth that we were able to distill from the excellent-companies research. We might be tempted to reply, "Figure out your value system. Decide what your company stands for."*

Perhaps the most important factor in corporate success is a set of driving values directing management decisions. The basic beliefs at IBM, the Johnson & Johnson Credo, Motorola's striving for technical perfection, the Delta family feeling and 3M's belief in product innovation are a few examples of the driving values that lead excellent companies.

Dr. Robert Schuller, best-selling author and possibility thinker, wrote these words many years ago:

> *Sam is fifty-six years old. All his life he has—sometimes mildly, sometimes severely—hated himself. Why? Listen as he sits in my study and pours out his story. "All my life I've tried to be somebody else. I never dared to be me. I didn't think I was good enough. So I've been a phony for over half a century. That's the trouble with people—they're all trying to be somebody else, and that's impossible!"* [2]

Schuller adds:

> *We strive desperately to keep our real self a secret, even from ourselves. The possibility of self-disclosure is frighten-*

ing to most people. We do all kinds of things to cover up. Clothes, cars, and cosmetics are frequently masks that we put on to try to kid ourselves and others. Be honest enough to dare to allow your real self to be unveiled. Stop hiding behind fear of exposure, fear of rejection or a fear of seeing a failing personality. Don't ignore the opportunity to know yourself well enough to improve yourself. [3]

Everyone is guided by values, regardless of whether those values are recognized. It is crucial to assess and to constantly reassess the values being reflected in one's actions.

KNOW YOURSELF

Before you can lead others, you must learn to lead yourself. Speaking of corporate values is fine, but what are your values.

The idea of a value system, for individuals and for organizations, is a powerful idea. Leaders and visionary companies are aware of the power of a well-defined value system.

As outlined in Chapter 2, a value is a cherished idea. Once one's value system is clarified, it provides focus. By contrast, people who seem to have no direction are typically those without a guiding purpose or a coherent set of deep beliefs.

The differences between non-values-based and values-based people are obvious. People without a clarified value system tend to look only at results that can be easily measured—an "A" or "B" grade in school, a college degree, shooting a 72 in golf, a job title. Values-based people, by contrast, seem to express their core beliefs in quality terms—educational pursuits, enjoyment, innovation, personal growth, self-esteem and satisfaction.

Therefore, the most important concept leaders can bring to organizations may well be their efforts to clarify their personal values.

VALUES SELF-CHECK

In a notebook, write a complete sentence for each of the following phrases. Work rapidly, writing down the first thing that pops into your mind.

(1) My greatest priorities in life are:

(2) My best talents, personally and professionally, are:

(3) My life is:

(4) Ten years from now, where will I probably live?

(5) Ten years from now, what will I be doing?

(6) Ten years from now, what assets will I own?

(7) Ten years from now, will I be happy?

(8) More than anything, I want:

How can you begin to identify your value system? I have developed the *values self-check*, which appears in the box above. Let me suggest that you obtain a spiral notebook which you can use while reading the remainder of *The Heart of Business*. You will have several more opportunities to write your thoughts or answer specific questions, beginning with this Self-Test.

How do you feel about your answers?

What do your sentences say about your hopes for the future?

DESIRE FOR VALUES

Look at your answer to the last question: "More than anything, I want _____." Whatever you wrote in that blank, may I ask, how much do you want it?

Let me illustrate the "how-much?" question with a story:

A young man came to Socrates one day with an urgent request. "I have walked 1,500 miles to gain wisdom and learning," the student began. "I want learning, so I came to you. Can you give it to me?"

Socrates spoke without hesitation: "Come, follow me."

The acclaimed teacher led the student to the seashore. He walked into the gentle waves until he and his young follower were in water up to their waists.

Then Socrates grabbed his companion and pushed his head under the water. In spite of the younger man's frantic struggles, the teacher held him under.

After several tense moments, Socrates pulled the young man out of the water, laid the would-be pupil on the shore and returned to the marketplace.

When the young man regained his strength, he walked back to Socrates.

"You are a man of learning and wisdom," the young man challenged furiously. "Why did you treat me so badly?"

"When you were under the water," Socrates asked, "what was the one thing you wanted more than anything else?"

"I wanted air!"

Then Socrates said, "When you want wisdom and understanding as badly as you wanted air, you won't have to ask anyone to give it to you. You will get it wherever and whenever you can!"

How about you? If you could have whatever you want, what would it be? What would your life be like?

What do you desire: Stronger values? Peace of mind? To feel good about yourself? A sense of pride? Plenty of money? Recognition?

A recent Roper Report poll, based on interviews with several thousand American adults, pointed to six primary "what-do-I-want-out-of-life" dreams:

- The highest percentage, 86%, wanted to own a home. Of those polled, 60% had attained this dream.

- The next highest number, 77%, desired a happy marriage, but only 55% felt that they had reached this goal.

- Fewer than 75% listed owning a car as a desire—perhaps because this is so common today—and 82% already had completed this common transaction.

- 72% wanted to have children, and 62% had achieved this dream.

- 62% dreamed of having lots of money, but only 4% had reached that goal.

- 61% desired interesting jobs, but only one-third of those polled felt successful in this important pursuit. [4]

What does this say about values? Everybody, it seems, wants a measure of success. People generally want what they feel life can deliver. On that, most can agree.

But as long as you keep defining success by outside definitions, you will be largely unfulfilled.

I believe that your definition of success must come from within. I also believe that success means that you should have a vision reaching beyond where you are right now. But only you know what your values, goals and dreams include.

On several occasions I have formed values that have affected me for the rest of my life.

While I was studying in college in Indonesia, I was chosen to work for a multi-million-dollar United Nations development program. My job was to evaluate the economic impact of building and other infrastructure. I traveled to an Indonesian province with my American counterpart to manage a group of people.

In the late '60s, my counterpart from the United States received a salary of close to $40,000 a year, with all expenses paid. Since I was an Indonesian citizen, my salary had to be comparable to that of other Indonesian government employees—a few hundred dollars a year.

Since Indonesians performed work comparable to that performed by the well-paid Americans, we were encouraged to submit all expenses up to $3,000 a month for reimbursement. We were even encouraged to submit fictitious expenses up to that amount.

The local people treated me like a king. I stayed in the government guest house in the capital of the province. When I returned home, I had no additional expenses to report. I could have fabricated some expenses and become rich overnight, by Indonesian standards. I did some soul-searching and decided that I would live by the standards of honesty, integrity, courage and ethical conduct.

The decision cost me in the short term. Not only did I pass up a healthy infusion of cash, but also I had to leave this project. In the long run, though, my decision gave me the incentive to work hard for my success. I owe my success in the United States to my decision to stick to my values, no matter how hard it was in the beginning and no matter how difficult it seemed at the time.

Where do you want to be? More importantly, where are you right now?

TAKE RESPONSIBILITY

Having strong values is no accident. Success is no accident. Failure is no accident. Success or failure is the result of choices you have made and actions that you have taken.

In fact, there are no accidents. You alone are responsible for your choices—past, present and future. You are whatever you are because of what you have allowed through your mind in the past. Moreover, you will be tomorrow whatever you choose to be because of what you allow through your mind from this moment.

This is exciting information, because it is true, and because it is the key to your future. You are responsible for your choices.

VALUES SUMMARY

Values are absolutely vital to personal excellence. If you don't feel good about yourself, you will reject many of the good things which come to you. When enough people in any organization don't have clear values, the result is inevitable.

Writes Lee Iacocca:

I look around me and I see Wall Street executives being dragged away in handcuffs. I see a national deficit so high that I can't count the zeroes. I see the government paying farmers not to plant their land while the homeless go hungry on the streets. Something's rotten out there—and it's not in Denmark. [5]

The best-selling author and former Chrysler CEO insists:
The only way to get this country back on track is to return to good old-fashioned horse sense. We've got to start with the basics: how we raise our kids, how we care for our sick and homeless, what it is each of us truly believes. And we've got to remember what America stands for, so that we can take our tarnished values and make them shine again. [6]

Begin now by assessing the values that shape the way you treat other people, the values that control your approach toward life, the values that affect your attitude about excellence and quality, and the values that are already having impact on your future.

Take responsibility for your life right now. Develop your own clear set of values, and live by them.

Values to Remember

(1) For each of us there is a person who is standing just beyond an imaginary door—five years, 10 years, 20 years in the future.

(2) We all have values that guide us, regardless of whether those values are recognized consciously.

(3) It is crucial to assess and to constantly reassess the values being reflected in your actions.

(4) Before you can lead others, you must learn to lead yourself.

(5) You alone are responsible for your values and choices—past, present and future.

The unexamined life is not worth living.

SOCRATES (470-399 B.C.)
Greek Philosopher

PART II

READINESS OF THE HEART

Chapter 4

HOW TO ESTABLISH A POSITIVE VALUE BASE

Chapter 5

HOW TO TRANSLATE VALUES INTO PRACTICAL APPLICATIONS

Chapter 6

HOW TO CULTIVATE VALUES-BASED TEAMWORK

Chapter 7

HOW TO CLEAR AWAY NEGATIVE VALUES

FOUR

How to Establish a Positive Value Base

To be effective, a leader must develop relationships that establish the trust and common purpose necessary for sharing both sacrifices and gains. He or she must motivate and inspire a generation with new values and emotional attitudes, emphasizing enriching experience and self-development. [1]

MICHAEL MACCOBY
American Author

BUSY-NESS OR BUSINESS?

Henry David Thoreau, the 19th Century naturalist and author wrote: "It's not enough to be busy; so are the ants. The question is: What are we busy about?"

It's a fair question.

Thus far in Section I of this book, I have dealt with business and leadership challenges, the meaning of values and how to assess your own values.

In Section II, let me begin to translate individual values into the corporate setting.

"What are we busy about?"

Let me suggest a foundation of ABCs for values, success and long-term productivity: ATTITUDE, BELIEFS and COURAGE TO CHANGE.

ATTITUDE
B
C

What are the characteristics of any extraordinary, values-based achiever?

I often ask that question as I talk with my associates or clients. The answers are fairly predictable. A top performer is a person who is:

- Considerate of others
- Energetic
- Attentive to detail
- Highly self-confident
- Positive
- A good planner
- Open
- Creative
- Disciplined
- Persistent
- Diplomatic
- Imaginative
- Communicative
- Goal-oriented
- Concerned
- A visionary
- Respected a great deal

Maybe you can add even better descriptors to this list. If so, take a moment to write them in your notebook.

Now, look back at the list I've written, plus yours. Which attributes have anything to do with mechanical or technical skill? Few. Which ones are centered on attitude? Nearly all.

What is the message? Of the attributes an outstanding performer generally possesses, attitude continually is the most important component.

Goethe, the German philosopher, said: "They can because they think they can."

Likewise, King Solomon wrote: "As a man thinks in his heart, so is he."

Marcus Aurelius mused, "A man's life is what his thoughts make of it."

Ralph Waldo Emerson said this: "A man is what he thinks about all day long."

As you can see, wise people throughout history have disagreed on virtually every major philosophical thought, but on this point all great teachers have agreed: We are what we think about. Attitude is the key.

None of us has 100% control of circumstances in life. We can better ourselves, certainly. We can become more proficient in whatever skills we need. We can seek the best environment in which our talents can develop. But we still cannot predetermine a perfect situation every moment in life.

I learned to have a good attitude the hard way, for it took a tragedy to teach me that truth.

When I first learned of the illness that sent me to the hospital for 10 months as a teen-ager, I cried, "Why me?" The initial diagnosis by the doctor was very bad. I would probably not survive. At best, I would have to spend years in bed as an invalid.

At first, I believed that dying would be a better alternative than slowly wasting away. It was difficult enough in my native country to survive, even when a person was healthy. Subsisting in squalid, harsh situations as an invalid would be almost impossible.

My cherished childhood dream of going to the United States some day was crushed. I grew mad at God. I hated everybody. My body was wracked with pain. For months I could not make even the slightest movement without excruciating, white-hot pains shooting through my body.

I wondered for hours and days why life was treating me so cruelly. I felt that nobody cared. I tried to keep from panicking, from crying out, from going totally insane.

One of the things I could do, very carefully, was to read. I began devouring the dog-eared, yellowed pages of many inspirational and historical books, learning how the greatest men and women had become successful. I spent literally hundreds of hours studying the stories and teachings in the Bible.

A small radio that I was allowed to use became another wonderful companion. When I couldn't sleep, I could be transported beyond my pain through the voices that I heard—voices that truly became beacons in the night. I reveled in the soothing, calming music.

Bedridden in a dank, windowless room, I was deprived of the pleasures of seeing or hearing the beauty of a creation I had taken for granted: rainbows, flowers, animals, towering shade trees, laughter of children, sunsets and sunrises, the fragrance of my native land's tropical flowers. I learned that my thoughts could take me farther than my eyes and ears.

It took many months, but my fears, worries and panic were transformed into heart-inspiring hope, courage and faith. God took control of my life. I learned to be patient, to surrender my life and problems to Him.

Ironically, though I was confined as an invalid, I began to experience life more fully than I had ever dreamed. I promised God that if I was ever given the opportunity to recover from my illness, I would serve Him, and I would never take life for granted again.

Despite the doctor's dire predictions and all outward signs, I started getting well. Many months later, I was able to walk again. Today, I am alive because of the miracle of a heart and attitude change.

We all have control over our thoughts. Out of our attitudes—bad or good—we create actions; out of actions, we create circumstances; and circumstances create beliefs. Attitudes are among the primary foundations for values. Values determine everything we become. Therefore, we each have control of a never-ending cycle that is propelled by beliefs and value-based decisions.

Webster's defines attitude as one's disposition, opinion, mental set; the position or posture assumed in connection with an action, feeling or mood.

We can choose every moment of every day what attitude we have. That applies to you and to every teammate in your organization.

ATTITUDE
BELIEFS
C

The most famous tightrope walker of the late 1890s was Charles Blondin. He conquered Niagara Falls as no man or woman has done since. To cross Niagara Falls by walking across a cable was a breathtaking feat in itself, but Blondin was able to:

- Cross the falls on four different occasions.

- Do a backward somersault at the middle of the Falls.

- Take a chair to the middle and sit on it, balancing the chair on two legs.
- Go across it on stilts.
- Walk across blindfolded while pushing a woman on a wheel-barrow.
- Stand on his head in the middle of the tightrope.
- Take a small stove half-way across, sit down, cook himself an omelette and eat it.

On one of those four occasions, 10,000 cheering, excited people from Canada and the U.S. appeared to watch the titan of the tightrope perform his awesome feat.

A tense cheer rose from both sides of the falls as he stepped onto the mist-slippery, torturously-thin strand. For four hours he inched from the Canadian side to the United States side, and the masses screamed louder. As he finally stepped from the cable, the people exploded in noise, chanting his name: "Blondin! Blondin! Blondin!"

He raised his arms to quiet the throng. When the crowd's noise sank to a whisper, he shouted dramatically, "I am Blondin. Do you believe in me?"

Thousands immediately roared as one voice, "We believe! We believe!"

He thundered, "To prove that I am the greatest—now and evermore—I will walk back across this tightrope."

The crowd gasped, then roared its approval.

He gestured for quiet once more, then continued, "This time I am going to carry someone on my shoulder. Do you believe I can do this?"

Without hesitation the men, women and children screamed, "We believe! We believe! We believe!"

He allowed the chanting to go on for some time. When it subdued, he looked over the audience and asked, "Who will be that brave person?"

Silence! Nobody said anything. It seemed as if no one breathed.

He repeated his question: "You believe in me—who will be that brave person who goes back with me?"

Again, more silence. After many heart-pounding minutes, one man stepped out of the crowd and silently climbed onto Blondin's shoulders. For the next four hours, the two men moved slowly back to the Canadian side of the falls.

Ten-thousand people had shouted, "We believe! We believe!" But only one had really acted on his belief.

Belief in ourselves, in God, or in others requires that we act on those beliefs. Believing moves far beyond wishing, or even hoping. It carries the conviction that will transform visions to realities.

How does the subject of beliefs fit into a book about business? Without it, we are a muddled, disheveled, defensive people.

In a values-based environment, all people should be able to contribute their beliefs freely, without having them stifled. In such a climate, leaders become encouragers of a shared vision. That is quickly recognized by the team.

Trusting people to be creative and constructive when given more openness does not imply an overoptimistic or Pollyanna-like belief in the flawlessness of human nature. Rather, it is a conviction that the errors and imperfections of any group of human beings are far better overcome by people working together in an environment of belief, vision, trust, freedom and mutual respect, than by men and women working under a crush of rules, regulations and restraints imposed on them by another group of all-too-imperfect people.

The shocking changes that have occurred since 1989 in Eastern Europe and the former Soviet Union provide the best proof of this. Nowhere else and at no other time, has the crumbling facade of totalitarianism been more exposed.

Why, then, do companies that should know better still attempt to force top-down controls? Few people are willing to accept that kind of rigid control anymore.

There is a place for belief, even in the sophisticated times in which we live—especially during these times.

ATTITUDE
BELIEF
COURAGE TO CHANGE

To lead a values-based organization forward, we have to have courage to face change—indeed, to thrive on it.

Values-founded leaders are rare in the marketplace today. Many managers and executives, who could become great leaders, instead become absorbed into safe, secure, riskless managerial situations.

That mindset requires dedication to processes, structures, roles, rules and indirect forms of communication. It discourages ideas, people, emotions and direct talk—the essence of true leadership.

Abraham Zaleznik, best-selling author and professor at Harvard Business School, calls this mindset "the managerial mystique." He writes:

> *The main credo of the managerial mystique is, act on form and hope that substantive solutions will follow. It selects attention from the realities of business. It calls on executives to relinquish their ability to think, and to adopt slogans and formulas instead of developing the art of self-examination that stimulate the imagination as well as toughen analytical thinking.*[2]

Zaleznik adds:

> *Leading is vastly different from managing. Leaders grow through mastering painful conflict during their developmental years, confronting experiences that cause them to turn inward. Managers, by contrast, perceive life as a steady progression of positive events, resulting in security at home, in school, in the community, and at work.*
>
> *Leaders are 'twice born' individuals who endure major events and crises that lead to a sense of separateness— estrangement—from their environment. They turn inward in order to re-emerge with a created, rather than inherited, sense of identity. The introspective capacity, which reinforces that sense of separateness, encourages deep thought about problems and methods for their solution.*[3]

So what does it take to effect sustainable changes in leaders and throughout any organization?

It takes courage to change, to be flexible, to take a chance and to put people above systems. Not many leaders have that depth.

VALUES SUMMARY

The finest organizations almost always have several key patterns flowing through involved individuals. These trends include an emphasis on personal performance and an environment that empowers the ABC foundations individual.

The ABC principle had a profound effect on the attitudes of Fred, one of my former employees.

Fred came to our company because he was discouraged with the bureaucracy in the large company where he held a relatively high position. A series of layoffs was imminent, and he decided to leave.

A series of setbacks had left him with a negative attitude. At first, he had risen very rapidly on the corporate ladder of another company. Then he quit to start his own business. The business failed, and he had to liquidate it and join a large company. Soon corporate politics and the stifling environment of the new company left him depressed.

During our working relationship, his belief in himself returned, and his courage to dream resurfaced. He was offered a very lucrative contract to head a start-up company in the bio-medical field, with a lot of incentives to make him a multi-millionaire in a short time if he became successful.

As this is written, he is well on his way.

Everything comes back to attitudes. Systems and processes may come and go, but a person's (and an organization's) attitudes, beliefs and courage to change are at the core of any values-based issue.

Values to Remember

(1) You can use a foundation of ABCs for values, success and long-term productivity.

(2) Of the attributes upon which people generally agree as describing an outstanding performer, *attitude* is invariably the common denominator.

(3) In a values-based environment, all individual should be able to contribute their beliefs freely, without having them stifled.

(4) To effect a values-based organization, we have to have courage to change—indeed, to thrive on it.

*Many ideas grow better when trans-
planted into another mind than in the
one where they sprang up.*

OLIVER WENDELL HOLMES
(1841-1935)
Associate Justice United States Supreme Court

FIVE

How to Translate Values into Practical Applications

The purpose of freedom is to create it for others.
BERNARD MALAMUD

SHARED LEARNING

Even though I own several businesses and keep very busy with my consulting schedule, I am very much a family man. Except when I am traveling, I try religiously to spend several hours a day with my wife and children, doing things that they want to do.

Recently, I was walking along with my kids. We were doing nothing special—just spending time together.

One of my children said, "You know, Dad, when I grow up, I want to be just like you."

Magic words!

Then the other child said, "Yeah, Dad—me, too."

But I caught them off-guard. I beamed at them, happy at their words, then I said, "But you don't understand. When I grow up, I want to be just like you."

My statement was more than an attempt to join the Mutual Admiration Society. I was deeply serious. I have found that I always learn more from so-called subordinates than they learn from me.

I always want it to be that way.

PEOPLE EMPOWERMENT

The greatest challenge for any values-based leader is to become a catalyst, rather than a commander; a people-stretcher, rather than a people-pusher; and an empowerer, not a director.

The word "people" is central to values-based leadership, for it is the core of tomorrow's marketplace. As the world becomes more and more of a service-oriented economy (more about that in Chapter 9), and as the work force becomes more synergistic (more about that in Chapter 11), leaders can no longer hide in their ivory towers. True leaders must realize the necessity of attracting and retaining talented, innovative, committed employees.

Gone are the days when everyone was more or less expendable. Given the huge investment in recruiting and keeping the best employees, empowering must calculate success on a formula of stability and growth.

To assure stability and growth, leaders must devote resources toward personal growth. Buying-in has already become the corporate watchword.

Joe D. Batten, in his book, *Tough-Minded Leadership*, writes:

The new leader will cultivate flexibility, mental suppleness, and resilience. Rigid thinking and defensive action have no place in the tool box of the new leader. [1]

Batten adds:

Peak performers—winners—are motivated by passionate commitment to a transcendent vision, dream or mission. [2]

This will happen only when an organization is able to infuse individuals with three significant values:

- A deep motivation to succeed;

- A vision of what can happen in the future;

- Widespread buy-in by team members into the motivation and belief.

Let's take these values one at a time.

MOTIVATION

Webster's describes motivation as "an inner drive, impulse or that which causes one to act in a certain way." Motivation, simply stated, is a personal reason to succeed.

A dynamic motivation is perhaps the most striking characteristic of a values-based organization. Clearly, an overriding purpose or mission is the basis for any strategic planning, but it is even more important that a vivid organizational motivation become the basis for shared meaning among employees.

I have seen success come to my company and many other companies when their people discovered the mission.

One of those companies was IMMAC, founded by Ken Eldren, who started it in his garage 10 years ago. IMMAC specializes in mail-order distribution of computer accessories. The company prided itself on rapid delivery and quick turn-around of merchandise.

Ken started with a mission that incorporated honesty, integrity and insistence on what is right for the customer. He applied Christian principles to his daily life and involved his employees in the accomplishment of his mission. Today his personal net worth is close to $60 million.

Another friend, Jamie Farris, single-handedly transformed a floundering branch office of one of the top three tax-preparing companies. She was given responsibility for straightening out problems that had many employees on the verge of quitting **en masse**.

Her boss recommended that she fire everyone and start with all new employees. Higher management was convinced that the problem was so monumental it couldn't be solved.

Farris started by securing the cooperation of the former branch manager, who had been demoted. Then she began transforming the employees into a unit of hard-working individuals. She gave them a mission: to become the best in customer service, in profitability and in employee participation.

She changed the attitudes from negative to positive almost overnight by motivating the people from within. She helped create personal motivation by treating employees like adult humans, praising them whenever she caught them doing something right.

Sincere praise instead of criticism turned that branch into one of the largest and fastest-growing branches in the company.

Farris succeeded by paying attention to something that is often overlooked by modern managers. For all of the importance placed today upon strategic planning, mission statements, and organizational culture, leaders and consultants frequently ignore motivation. Instead, we talk about goals. Goals are wonderful, but unless the reason for existing is established first, goals tend to allow hidden conflicts to go unresolved.

Equally important, goals can be achieved without attaining the deep fulfillment that comes from realizing a highly-valued motivation.

Tommy Lasorda, manager of the world champion Los Angeles Dodgers and three-time National League manager of the year says:

> *Winning the World Series in 1988 was positive proof of what you can obtain in life if you really believe in yourself. Those 24 players got together and all believed in themselves, and what they did last year showed. It captured the hearts of America because it showed that it is not always the strongest man that wins the fight. In most cases it's the one who wants it just a little bit more than the next, and that's what this team did last year. They wanted it more.* [3]

An internally generated motivation can give powerful direction. Then, and only then, can you establish external goals that are mileposts for accomplishing what motivates you.

Everything begins with asking, "What is our true reason for existing—our motivation?" Nothing else can make sense unless your people agree on this matter.

VISION

Vision, while used many times as a synonym for motivation , is actually much deeper. It flows out of purpose. Peter Block, for example, defines vision as:

> *Our deepest expression of what we want. It is the preferred future, a desirable state, an ideal state, an expression of optimism. It expresses the spiritual and idealistic side of our nature. It is a dream created in our waking hours of how we would like our lives to be.*

Webster's defines vision as a mental image.

Regardless of the technical definition, any organization's vision stems from the inner motivation and collective values of its individuals. These aspirations should include such areas as personal growth, corporate excellence and service to others.

Vision has many facets. It:
* Inspires people to reach for what could be.

- Helps men and women to rise above their fears and preoccupations with what can go wrong.

- Gets them to think beyond what currently exists.and what they really want, independent of what seems possible now.

- Motivates people far more effectively than a problem-oriented mindset, because it is not bound by preconceived limitations.

- Provides an unlimited horizon.

- Enables people to clarify and realize what they really want, independent of what seems possible now.

- Encourages them to develop a vision of their ideal and then builds a bridge between the current and desired states.

Moving toward visionary goals will require problem-solving, of course, but the solutions are likely to be less limiting, more effective and more satisfying than with a problem-oriented mindset.

BUY-IN

Buy-in implies ownership, and ownership implies unified movement. Once a values-based organization develops clarity in motivation and vision, it can be infused with life and vitality.

Teams that buy in are more likely to get along. The members generally keep their agreements with one another because of their commitments to an overriding motivation and vision.

Unified, values-based employees are also more capable of both disagreeing about ideas and resolving those disagreements because of their deep, unifying commitment.

John Sculley, in his best-selling book, **Odyssey**, talks about the concept already in place when he moved from Pepsi to Apple Computers:

> *At Apple, we promote "buy-in management," a group decision-making process that recognizes individuals regardless of where they reside in the company. This was quite a difference from the "top-down management" style of so many American corporations, in which the boss simply issues an order from the top and the troops below*

meekly follow the command. It also was different from Japanese-styled "consensus management," which allows for a consensus of support to build in favor of a decision in an orderly fashion within the organization. Consensus often means a company is willing to adopt the "average" if everyone accepts it.

Buy-in, however, doesn't allow for compromise. If someone has an idea, he or she is obligated to sell and persuade others that it's important. Ideas and decisions in a buy-in company can originate anywhere—not from the top down as they do in many second-wave U.S. corporations, nor bubbling up through a rigid hierarchical structure as in Japanese companies.

Buy-in encourages unfettered group discussion of attitudes, policies, and ideas. [4]

Developing buy-in through motivation and vision is a primary values-based foundation because it is an important condition for building effectiveness. Once people are unified, it is easier for them to make agreements and to foster working environments that will help everyone achieve their shared dreams. That, in a very real sense, is the purpose of *The Heart of Business*.

VALUES SELF-CHECK

In the notebook you are using for your notes, write a complete sentence (only one!) for each of the following phrases. Write the first thing that pops into your mind.

(1) My company's reason for existing is:

(2) My company's vision for the future is:

(3) My role in helping my company reach our goals is:

(4) The values I want my company to have are:

(5) I want my company's working environment to be:

(6) Buy-in exists/does not exist in my company because:

(7) I have achieved:

(8) My personal purpose in reaching my team's goals is:

(9) I am accomplishing:

(10) People on my team are:

How do you feel about your answers?
What do your sentences say about your hopes for the future?

VALUES SUMMARY

A shared motivation and vision, and therefore, buy-in, must come from the inner heart of any organization.

Let us illustrate with a classic story: Three men were at a work site laying brick. All three had the same tools, mortar of identical consistency and materials that were alike. Yet they looked different as they worked. An observer went to each one.

"What are you doing?" the questioner asked the first worker.

"Layin' brick," the laborer grumbled. "It's a paycheck, even if it is hard work."

"What are you doing?" the observer asked the next man.

"Well," the second worker replied, "I'm one of the construction people, and we are putting together the east wall of a structure."

"What are you doing?" the questioner asked the third worker.

"I am helping to build a cathedral," he wiped his brow and spoke excitedly. He gestured, "And someday, right where we are standing, the spires will rise high above us, and people will be meeting to worship and be educated."

The first worker worked to get a paycheck. The second man had an idea of the company's goals. The third man had bought into a powerful motivation and vision.

TAKING THE TIME TO ACHIEVE BUY-IN

Soon after we started our company, we experienced tremendous growth. We hired new people as we received new projects. We had to hire many highly skilled professional people for one project. The project had to be executed quickly, with many tight deadlines. We had to acquire competency without delay.

We didn't have time for training. When the project started, the project manager was not a strong person. As a result, people began working in different directions. People were working on the basis of different ideas, and individuals were doing things their own way. The result was chaos.

In a management meeting, we asked the people to stop working, even though we had deadlines. We felt it was important that we all have the same mind. We gathered everyone together and explained our mission, emphasizing that we needed their help to come up with a plan for proceeding with the project.

We encouraged their comments and acknowledged their suggestions. Although it took four hours of heavy discussion, we emerged with a plan of action whereby all hands knew what was expected of them and what their individual contributions would be.

Had we failed to bring that project in on time, the client would have lost millions of dollars. We made it on time, and the client was so pleased that we were awarded a contract on another project.

Without buy-in from all, we would not have been able to succeed. As Warren Bennis and Burt Nanus write in **Leaders**:

A vision cannot be established in an organization by edict, or by the exercise of power or coercion . . . In the end, the leader may be the one who articulates the vision and gives it legitimacy, who expresses the vision in captivating rhetoric that fires the imagination and emotions of followers, who—through the vision—empowers others to make decisions that get things done. But if the organization is to be successful, the image must grow out of the needs of the entire organization and must be 'claimed' or "owned" by all the important actors. [5]

Within every organization lies the potential not only for success, but also for greatness. Collective commitment to the highest in ourselves and others makes the vital difference in nurturing this greatness into reality. These exciting results can only come through a shared motivation, a clear vision and buy-in.

Values to Remember

(1) I have found that I always learn more from so-called subordinates than they learn from me.

(2) The greatest challenge for any values-based leader is to become a catalyst, rather than a commander; a people-stretcher, rather than a people-pusher; and an empowerer, not a director.

(3) Great results happen when an organization is able to infuse individuals with three significant values:
- A deep motivation.
- A vision of what the organization stands for or strives to create.
- Buy-in to that motivation and vision by team members.

(4) A motivation and vision, and therefore, buy-in, must come from the inner heart organization.

"Let your value system guide you. Your goals must be compatible or they will be combatible. Unless they are compatible with your own deepest value system, they will be combatible. Then you will have tension, guilt and anxiety inside of you and you won't be able to succeed." [6]

ROBERT H. SCHULLER
Best-selling author and minister

SIX

How to Cultivate Value-Based Teamwork

Teamwork is essential for a productive organization. Collaboration is needed to develop the commitment and skills of employees, solve problems, and respond to environmental pressures. Fostering collaboration is not just a nice idea. It is the key that leaders use to lock the energies and talents available in their organization. [1]

JAMES M. KOUZES and
BARRY Z. POSNER
Best-selling authors

VALUES-BASED LEADERSHIP

Conventional thinking, based on the boss/hired-hand mindset, tends to stifle initiative, creativity, innovation and teamwork. A values-based environment, however, energizes and promotes everyone within the organization.

How? Here are 10 quick reasons:

(1) *Ownership*

Ownership is a special condition created when people see their organization's purpose as an extension of their personal purposes. When employees emotionally and consciously "buy" into an organization's goals, they also assume responsibility for the company's success by embracing the vision as their own and by sharing accountability for achieving it.

(2) *Networking*

John Naisbitt was one of the first to define networking in his runaway best-selling *Megatrends*:

> *"Simply stated, networks are people talking to each other, sharing ideas, information, and resources. The point is often made that networking is a verb, not a noun. The important part is not the network, the finished product, but the process of getting there—the communication that creates the linkages between people and clusters of people. Networks exist to foster self-help, to exchange information, to change society, to improve productivity and work life, and to share resources. They are structured to transmit information in a way that is quicker, more high-touch, and more energy-efficient than any other process we know.* [2]

Our high-tech world has created a great need for high-touch relationships. Any business that ignores the desire for interaction—inside and outside the corporate boundaries—is destined to fail.

(3) *Communication*

Traditional structures, including physical locations and middle management's desire to use information as a power tool, thwart good corporate communication flow.

In the fast-paced, high-tech business world, these established patterns will be discarded in favor of flexible frameworks (primarily computerized systems) that facilitate the expeditious flow of information.

(4) *Swift response*

In the coming years, these flexible frameworks will be even more vital in enabling quick corporate responses to marketplace changes.

A look at today's business headlines shows numerous examples of leading companies that have learned the hard way that frustrated customers become ideal prospects for the competition.

Today's flatter systems have created a greater need for vital decisions among leaders who work in customer-close locations. Sluggish decision-making procedures mean lost opportunities.

(5) *Value-added service*

Service is no longer just a by-product of business; more and more, it *is* the business.

"The value of quality service is phenomenal," observed Joshua Hammond, publisher of *The Quality Review*, pointing to the fact that top-notch value was the primary reason such marketplace champions as L. L. Bean, American Express and Nordstroms were growing about twice as fast as other companies in their fields.

The area of value-added service is clearly the most neglected and avoided in American business (more about this in Chapter 9).

(6) *Innovation*

Companies are increasingly challenged to search for better procedures, merchandizing and services. Accelerated changes in the marketplace have created the absolute necessity for better innovation. Values-based leaders can never stop urging, "Let's find a better way to do this."

(7) *Self-discipline*

Whereas outmoded corporate structures depend on authoritarianism, values-based companies develop self-actuated discipline.

Peter Drucker has said repeatedly: "The information-based organization will function only if each individual and each unit accepts responsibility—for their goals and priorities, for their relationships and for their communications." [3]

(8) *Worker empowerment*

Traditional companies urge, "Do your job and help the company do well." Values-based leadership attracts the most talented innovators by pledging, "If the company does better than expected, and if you do a great job, we will all do well!"

Also, as John Naisbitt expressed it in Megatrends 2000, technology has paved the way for the empowerment of the individual. Unlike so many "big brother" scenarios, advances in technology have actually caused individualism to run rampant. [4]

(9) *Passion for quality*

Values-based corporations must set new standards of excellence—from top leaders to front-line team-members. (more about this in Chapter 10).

(10) *Excitement about change*

Change must be seen as beneficial, creating a win-win situation for everyone. One of the greatest challenges for today's leaders is to help employees who have become accustomed to functioning in large, impersonal, bureaucratic conglomerates, to understand the meaning of creative corporate freedom.

Only when people buy into the company's purpose and understand the meaning of their contributions to the organization's overall success, will change be seen as necessary and beneficial.

How can you succeed as a values-based leader? Start by being increasingly aware of the necessity for true teamwork. If ever corporations needed value-conscious, quality-minded, service-oriented, team-minded leaders, that time is now.

TEAMWORK

"Leadership," said Lou Holtz, head football coach of the national champion Notre Dame Fighting Irish, "is getting a group of people to move in a direction toward a worthwhile goal."

Patricia Carrigan, plant manager for General Motors, believes in teamwork. She says:

> *Working together in democratic fashion on a day-to-day basis proves to be the hardest thing most of us ever do. It gets easier as trust grows and mutual respect deepens— and as all can see the payoff.*

Everyone should know the importance of working together, right? We've been inundated with "If-we-all-pull-together" cliches since childhood. Superbowl quarterbacks smile into television cameras and say, "I couldn't have thrown that winning pass without my offensive line—they are the real heroes." Olympic medalists laud their coaches and the encouragement of the crowd.

The team concept works well in athletics. Business is also beginning to see the importance of team spirit. It is critical for you, as a values-based leader, to develop a teamwork mentality.

THE MONDAVI TEAM

Robert Mondavi of the Mondavi winery believes in teamwork. His family has been in the wine business in California's Napa Valley since 1919. His wife, Margaret Beaver, is credited with bringing international recognition not only to Mondavi wines but also to the Napa Valley wine country.

Using the team concept, Mondavi recognizes the value of each employee. Every year, the winery sends about 20 employees to tour the wine country of France so they will further understand the wine-making process. Mondavi seeks employee input. He gives each of his employees a case of the new wine, requesting their opinions.

Teamwork wasn't one of the founding principles of the Mondavi winery. Mondavi learned its value through experience. He had two sons and a daughter in the business. Mike, the oldest son, handled the market sales while Tim was the wine-maker in charge of production. Daughter Marcy, represented the winery in Europe and New York.

At first, Robert Mondavi tried to control the operation alone, not communicating with the others. His managers, relying on Bob for direction, would not make decisions on their own. Sibling rivalries developed among the three children. Suddenly, Bob Mondavi, at the age of 70, realized that his management team wasn't functioning at all.

He concluded that he needed to step away from the business and give the others authority to make decisions. He also needed to let them engage in team building.

Bob Mondavi stopped giving orders and became the mentor. He created a management council, rotating the chairmanship among the six corporate officers. While empowering his team, Bob didn't stop expecting the best from his people, but he revised his primary expectation of them. He stopped condemning people when they didn't perform the way he expected. He no longer focused on how his employees reached their goals; instead, he encouraged them to chart their own paths toward their goals, and he made himself available when they needed his advice and counsel.

THE POWER OF TEAM BUILDING

A colleague and I once led a team-building exercise at a resort area in Paharo Dunes for a group of key executives from a large company in that area. The executives realized that lack of teamwork had almost led to failure in developing a new software product.

They had hired a lot of people and were determined to complete the large project in 18 months instead of the five years it would normally take.

A lot of bright people were hired, but they never wanted to communicate with each other. When they failed—as inevitably they would—each blamed the other person.

My friend and I helped them establish a detailed set of milestones leading toward successful completion of the project. Then we helped them to see the necessity of team building.

We used a number of instruments to determine the learning styles and behavior styles of the people involved with the project. Once they understood that each person had a certain way of doing things, and that individual behaviors were not intended to conflict with the goals of the other people, they started to cooperate.

These exercises, along with physical exercises and midnight fireplace meetings helped them to become friends.

They understood the power of team building when they realized how much easier it was to establish the milestones through teamwork.

LEVERAGE

How do you unlock your team's energies and talents? The answer: *leverage.*

Archimedes once said, "Give me a lever and I can move the world." Leverage is most powerful when used with people.

The late J. Paul Getty, one of the richest men in history, once said, "If you help enough people get what they want, you will automatically get what you want."

The values-based leader—one who understands human needs and who can relate the goals and plans of an organization to fulfillment of all employees' needs—is the leader who will achieve the greatest success in reaching goals, both collectively and individually.

The key to leverage is learning to read people.

HOW TO READ PEOPLE

Getting along with others is hard enough. Cooperation is even more difficult. Getting people to help you reach your goals can prove nearly impossible—unless you learn to read body language.

But you can collaborate with others. In fact, unless you decide to become a hermit or pole-sitter instead of a leader, your success will largely depend on your people-skills.

Consider three of the best ways you can read your teammates better (also use these points as a self-check to see what signals you are sending):

(1) *Discern body language.*

Learn to assess each team member's attitude by combining both verbal and body language cues. Total feedback is the key to reading any person.

Here are five simple examples of unspoken signals:

- *Analysis clues*

    Nodding, eyeglass earpieces in mouth, hand on chin, finger to mouth and good eye contact—these are often indicators that a person is either in agreement with you or is carefully thinking through what you're saying.

- *Control clues*

    An aggressive attitude, confidence, and even superiority are suggested by intensive eye contact, touching fingertips, breathing restlessly, impatient fidgeting with hands (not to be confused with handwringing, as in the uncertainty clues) and sitting with hands behind the head. Other clear indications may be consciously standing while the other person sits or sitting while others in the room are standing.

- *Uncertainty clues*

    Poor eye contact, handwringing, fidgeting, bowed head, throat clearing and twitching are reliable indications that a person is nervous or insecure. Uncertainty or submissiveness may also be shown by cleaning one's glasses, putting a pencil in one's mouth, head scratching or head down—basically doing anything to avoid confrontation or to establish meaningful contact.

72

- *Challenge clues*
  When a person's body is angled noticeably toward or away from you, when the face is tense or arms akimbo—these are usually clear indications of skepticism, disagreement or even anger. A red face may indicate some form of challenge—hostility or unbelief.

- *Boredom clues*
  Disinterest or the doldrums can take many forms. Among the most obvious are a blank stare, looking out the window, fiddling with desk items, ring twisting, pencil percussion, shuffling papers, picking at clothing and foot tapping.

(2) *Listen intensively—not only to what people say, but to how they say it.*

Archie Bunker is a good example of a poor listener. He once said, "You know, Edith, the problem with our communication is that I speak in English, while you listen in dingbat!"

Listening (and all communication) must come from a genuine desire to hear the other person's point of view, as opposed to playing verbal volleyball or just wanting to be right.

You can turn the word LISTEN into an acronym that will help you lead each person in your organization into making a contribution to the team effort. Listening encourages people to buy in.

To **L-I-S-T-E-N**, follow these guidelines:

Look at the persons with whom you talk. Be aware of their facial expressions and body language.

Involve yourself in the conversation by saying:
"That's interesting."
"I know what you mean."
"Then what happened?"

Steady yourself, no matter what the other person says or does. If you maintain calm and keep listening, you can provide balance.

Translate the meanings of other people's remarks. Read between the lines so you can better understand what their needs are.

Excursions are taboo. Tune-in to the speaker. Boring people are easily distracted. Never interrupt the prospect.

Needs are paramount. Be concerned with the buyer's desires, and balance those needs with your personal and corporate interests.

When all leaders do is "get in their two cents' worth" by talking about their own interests, projects, and plans, they will undoubtedly encounter strong resistance.

The person who listens more in any conversation ultimately exerts a greater control on the final outcome of the discussion.

One point to remember: God gave you two eyes and two ears, but he gave you only one mouth. We should all take the hint. You automatically read people better when you talk less.

(3) *Be discerning with what you are told.*

When you read and listen to members of your team, be careful what you do with that information. Mark H. McCormack, author of the best-seller, ***What They Don't Teach You at Harvard Business School***, and founder of the International Management Group, wrote:

> *The idea of using what you have learned properly is not to tell them how insecure you think they are or to point out all the things you have perceptively intuited that they may be doing wrong. If you let them know what you know, you will blow any chance of using your own insight effectively.*

People don't like to have information used against them later, nor does anyone appreciate it when confidentialities are breached. The entire thrust of reading your team-members is to foster communication and mutually satisfying fulfillment.

The word ***communication*** means to cause a common action. Reading people better is not only the basis for all good team communication, but is also a key element of values-based leadership.

IGNITING TEAM SPIRIT

The concept of teamwork is not a passing fad. The team concept is one that will continue to move beyond lip service and participatory management, and eventually into areas of across-the-board synergism and creativity.

Yet backward-looking people often say, "The team `thing' is a good idea, but it promotes mediocrity, if not total chaos." I've even heard about a manager who said, "The team concept does two things: It drains energy from the winners, and it give an equal voice to losers."

In my opinion, nothing could be farther from the truth. The team leadership style does not abdicate authority, but it advocates group strength over boss/hired hand domination.

The best values-based leaders reach higher levels of success because they become proficient in motivating people and getting people to help accomplish mutually-satisfying goals.

This dynamic spirit can be ignited through leaders who understand five specific teamwork principles:

(1) *Give others what they want first*.

People will generally work harder for emotional benefits and recognition than they will for monetary income.

In any conversation, when possible, steer the discussion toward the person's needs and wants. People tend to support what they help create.

(2) *Show respect to others*.

In a *USA Today* poll, 100 managers across the nation were asked: *"What do you consider to be the biggest breach of business etiquette?"* The tally: [5]

- Miscellaneous answers—6%.
- Being late for appointments—6%.
- Off-color jokes or inappropriate humor—15%.
- Not giving others an opportunity to express themselves—28%.
- Criticizing a subordinate in front of others—45%.

Modeling is the first and, in many ways, the most important part of values-based leadership. Before you can reasonably expect to lead others successfully, you must lead yourself effectively. After all, a leader's own self-leadership behavior serves as a powerful model for followers. The example a leader sets can overshadow most other ways information is transmitted to team members about appropriate behavior.

(3) *Make people feel important.*

Human-resource professionals insist that as many as 90% of the things we do in life are fueled by a desire to feel important. Find avenues to have each person's unique talents contribute to overall team success. Seek genuine ways to be a team cheerleader, not just a coach.

(4) *Offer positive feedback.*

The human psyche seems to move and feed on praise, affirmation and attention.

All of us are still children, hardened a bit around the edges. We never really grow out of a constant need for praise and appreciation.

William James, one of the world's best-known psychologists, once said, "The desire to be appreciated is one of the deepest drives in human nature."

If your team members want praise (they do!), send lots of positive signals to their *WII-FM?* (What's In It For Me?) receiver. Become a skillful champion at back-patting and praise-giving.

(5) *Do simple favors for others.*

The Harvard Business School conducted an extensive test to determine how successful people earn the respect and cooperation of their co-workers. They found that one of the most effective techniques—developing a knack for doing simple favors—was also the easiest and least costly. You can become very creative at this in any environment.

(6) *Use names.*

Teach by example. Don't call your team-members "Hey, you!"

The sweetest sound in all the world is the sound of your own name. People get enough abuse during the normal day, so they will develop powerful feelings for a leader who makes the extra effort to remember and use the names they prefer.

Above all, have fun with your team. Sure, you have a job to do. Of course, you each have a role to play. But life is too short to see work as a series of mindless, thankless tasks.

Few leaders have held more responsible, demanding positions than Harold Geneen, the man who turned a faltering ITT into a giant conglomerate dealing in everything from Wonder Bread to Avis cars (while sales skyrocketed from $766 million to $22 billion). In describing how he built such excellence in team spirit, Geneen said:

> *I wanted to create an invigorating, challenging, cre-*
> *ative atmosphere at ITT. I wanted to get the people there to*
> *reach for goals that they might think were beyond them. I*
> *wanted them to accomplish more than they thought was*
> *possible. And I wanted them to do it not only for the*
> *company and their careers, but also for the fun of it. I*
> *wanted them to enjoy the process of tackling a difficult*
> *piece of business, solving it, and going on to bigger, better,*
> *and tougher challenges. I wanted them to do this, not for*
> *self-aggrandizement, but as part of a greater team effort, in*
> *which each player realized his own contribution to the*
> *team, knew that he was needed and appreciated, and took*
> *pride and self-satisfaction from playing a winning game.* [6]

Lighten up! Everyone winds up a winner by sharing positive, team-spirit attitudes with others in a creative, fun atmosphere.

THE TEAMWORK BARGAINING TABLE

Granted, the outdated boss/hired-hand mentality produced no problems with bargaining and negotiating between managers and workers. "My way or the highway" became the pervasive motto.

But that was yesterday. A values-based leader must become a master negotiator. Anytime more than one person is involved with anything, there must be allowances made for compromise and negotiation. A synergistic team, especially, must understand this principle.

"Everyone negotiates something every day," says Roger Fisher, director of the Harvard Negotiation Project at Harvard Law School. "You discuss a raise with your boss. You try to agree with a stranger on a price for his house. You negotiate with your spouse about where to go for dinner and with your child about when the lights go out."

Follow these four simple principles which are used not only in my companies, but can be applied by anyone works with people:

(1) *Think of negotiation as collaboration, not competition.*

When you think of life as "a jungle out there," it usually becomes a jungle. Win-or-lose approaches guarantee that at least one side will lose. Often, both do.

The collaboration (win-win) approach seeks solutions that will benefit both sides. In a good negotiation, whether in the executive office or during a sandlot football game, every participant should win something.

(2) *Separate the people involved from the problem.*

Don't let relationship issues cloud the matter being negotiated. Keep reaffirming the problem and solutions, not personal ramifications. Ideally, both parties should be discussing needs of each side.

(3) *Negotiate on the basis of needs, not positions.*

When both sides take positions—executive against manager, manager against front-line employee—they often defend those positions as if they were the real issues. Negotiation then disintegrates to mere haggling and attempting to save face.

Victor Kiam is a master at negotiation. He is the man who bought Remington, and within one year engineered a turnaround unprecedented in corporate history—tripling the company's sales and doubling its market share. Says Kiam:

> *Too many negotiations go down the tubes because of greed or self-centeredness. As a negotiator, you can wound yourself whenever you are overly concerned with what you need to get out of the transaction. You should back off. Your needs are a given; you're already close to them. If you've done your research, you should already know what your bottom line is and will recognize immediately when a deal is unacceptable to you. What you have to ascertain is what the other person hungers for.* [7]

(4) *Be creative with possible solutions.*

Good negotiators are often able to come up with unexpected, surprising ways to narrow the gap between differing positions. This can certainly happen with creative team members.

It takes two to make an argument. But it also takes at least two—working together—to complete a successful negotiation. Others can make excuses for deadlocks, but you, as the leader, must find mutually-satisfying ways to negotiate.

VALUES SUMMARY

There are only three ways to get anything done:
- Do it yourself.
- Get help.
- Give help.

Values-based leaders build powerful teams by combining those methods. Studies have shown that those who achieve outstanding success have generally done so by expanding and leveraging their efforts through others.

My company's experience with Greg provides an excellent example. Greg was an engineer with an excellent technical background who worked under one of my subordinates as our company was growing.

My subordinate praised him highly, and I concurred in the praise. He wanted to promote Greg to a managerial position. But despite Greg's technical expertise, we knew that many of his co-workers would be hurt by the promotion. They told us that they wouldn't work for Greg. They considered him to be judgmental and unforgiving—a man who demanded perfection when perfection was unattainable and who was harsh with people who failed to measure up to his impossible standards.

We understood that he was a technical genius, but had not developed good people skills.

My subordinate and I took Greg to lunch and discussed his job, his future, and his goals. Before joining our company, he had been steadily progressing in technical expertise, responsibility and salary. But he couldn't delegate, and he was not a good communicator. We communicated these concerns to him in a friendly way.

Greg opened up to us. He told us that his father had been a very successful businessman and had raised him according to the Protestant work ethic. He did whatever his father told him to do. In fact, Greg said, he feared his father until the day he died. He could still remember bringing home straight A's on his report card and hearing his father say, "Why not A+?" No matter what Greg did, it was never enough.

He tried to be the best in everything he did. People commented that he was too hard on himself; yet he couldn't stop.

We began to understand Greg's problem. He was really a perfectionist, hounded by a voice inside that kept saying, "You are not good enough yet; keep trying." This was the message his parents had conveyed to him. It was the message he was conveying to his co-workers. Greg seemed normal on the surface, but he was constantly straining to meet the unattainable expectations of his father. And he was trying to hold his co-workers to the same impossible standards.

We suggested that Greg make a list of the things he liked about himself and the things he wanted to be admired for. We asked him to list the characteristics of the person he would like to be associated with. As we ended the lunch, we asked him to practice more praise, more delegation, more compliments. We revealed our plan to promote him provided he could improve his human-relations skills.

After several months, Greg changed his attitude and he eventually became an excellent manager. He started showing empathy and asking questions. He even admitted to his employees that he was trying to improve his management skills, and asked them for suggestions.

Greg's subordinates already respected him for his technical expertise. Slowly he gained their respect as a boss.

The day Greg was promoted from acting manager to manager was a big day in his life. He continued to practice the art of delegating and leveraging himself by disseminating his technical knowledge and motivating his co-workers to achieve their work goals under his proficiency.

Greg's story illustrates that teamwork and the art of delegating are not necessarily inborn. Some people seem to be born with them, but Greg showed that they could be learned.

If you want to have a profound impact as a leader, develop the ability to believe in others. If you do, people will return your gift a thousand times.

Above all, remember Dale Carnegie's words:

You can make more friends in two months by becoming interested in other people than you can in two years by trying to get people interested in you.

That one teamwork- and values-based leadership principle could be the most important you will ever learn.

Values to Remember

(1) Conventional thinking, based on the boss/hired-hand mind-set, tends to stifle initiative, creativity, innovation and teamwork.

(2) A values-based environment, however, empowers and promotes everyone within the organization.

(3) How do you unlock your team's energies and talents? The answer: *leverage*.

(4) The key to leverage is to learn to read people.

(5) The best values-based leaders reach higher levels of success because they become proficient in motivating people and getting people to help accomplish mutually satisfying goals.

(6) It takes two to make an argument. But it also takes at least two—working together—to complete a successful negotiation.

"No great improvements in the lot of mankind are possible, until a great change takes place in the fundamental constitution of their modes of thought."

JOHN STUART MILL
English political economist
(1806-1873)

SEVEN

How to Clear Away Negative Values

At best, the current system of education prepares young people for pre-existing jobs in high-volume, standardized production. Some students are sorted into professional ranks and trained in the manipulation of abstract symbols. Others are prepared for lower-level routine tasks in production or sales. Few students are taught how to work collaboratively to solve novel real-world problems— the essence of flexible-system production. [1]

R. B. REICH
American Author

NEGATIVES

Often, the biggest challenge in communicating a new or clarified value base is to clear away all the negatives that are already inherent both in the organization, as a whole, and throughout the company, in individuals.

The human mind, unbridled, tends to the negative. The organizational mindset, unchallenged and unled, also seems to point naturally toward the negative.

Before discussing how to clear away negative values, however, let's look carefully at two specific problem areas: why leaders fail and why team members stumble.

WHY DO LEADERS FAIL?

Failure: It is every aspiring leader's nemesis. Whatever the reason for the failure, it is often easier to cover up past failures than to examine the reasons for them.

During my conversations with top executives, one"given" surfaces: Virtually all have suffered major misfortunes—from unfair work situations to missed promotions; from forced departures to highly publicized failures.

Of course, many unknowns can cause disaster: bad fortune, right time/wrong place, takeovers, one or more of the dreaded "isms" (sexism, ageism, racism).

More often, failure is self-related, rather than externally caused—usually through one of these six primary causes:

(1) *Poor interactive skills*

The inability to get along with others is the most widespread reason for the failures that I have seen—especially with employees in the early and middle stages of their careers.

Inability to get along with others is also the most debilitating deficiency individuals can detect and correct within themselves.

According to Robert Lefton, president of Psychological Associates Inc., a St. Louis consulting firm, weak managers typically can't inspire and win the loyalty of underlings because they aren't good listeners, don't give or take criticism well and "view conflict as something bad instead of something inevitable that has to be handled." [2]

(2) *Inability to be adaptable*

The inability to be resilient and to thrive on change is a fatal flaw, especially for those who insist on clinging to outmoded, mechanistic, top-to-bottom or dictatorial management styles.

Rigidity is also an increasingly dominant cause of failure for leaders in scores of corporations that have restructured, downsized or merged.

Too many leaders still insist, "Well, I don't care what anybody says—the old method worked in the past, and no one will ever make me change!"

(3) *Selfishness*

All leaders want to be recognized and rewarded for their efforts, but some are so preoccupied with individual corporate climbing that they become useless to the team.

Part of the blame, quite frankly, should be attributed to the success, power and leadership books, as well as the training systems that push one-upsmanship, aggressiveness and manipulation to extremes.

Says Cam Starrett, head of human resources for MacMillan, Inc.:

> *It's incredibly wearing to have to work with someone who's constantly demanding recognition and incapable of any selfless acts. Managers have to be authentic team players in today's leaner environment.* [3]

A large percentage of lonely-at-the-top leaders stumble because they cannot lead others unselfishly. Putting personal gain above their companies' most important needs is the worst offense. Sooner or later, as well-publicized downfalls have reiterated, narcissists somehow find a way to self-destruct.

(4) *Fear of failure*

Leaders may fail simply because they don't understand the value of occasionally failing. They may be limited by their inability to put themselves on the line. They may be diligent workers with new ideas but without the courage or conviction to sell them.

Such putative leaders try to prevent a fall by avoiding action—but in doing so actually accelerate their own ruin.

(5) *Lack of endurance*

There are many overnight successes who are unable to sustain their climb when faced with setbacks.

It is ironic that those who are unable to bounce back after failures often seem quite the same as those who have the ability to rebound.

Both groups are usually very bright and ambitious, but those who don't (or can't) recoup tend to react to failure by becoming defensive, trying to conceal it or blaming others.

By comparison, successful leaders almost always admit where they have erred and then try to correct their mistakes.

The way you handle failures and disappointments can often be the factor that makes or breaks your leadership climb.

Failures need not mark the end of your career, however. If you learn from your mistakes, your leadership breakdowns may prove to be your greatest assets.

(6) *Inability or unwillingness to support others*

I have seen hundreds of non-support situations that proved invariably detrimental to a team. Lack of support comes in many forms. It manifests itself primarily in the undermining of superiors, peers or subordinates.

Not nearly enough corporations foster support. Too often, their people are told, in essence, to watch their own backsides and never to get too supportive of anyone else.

These problems will not go away. Not enough companies have leaders with the value bases required to overcome these common failures.

WHY DO TEAM MEMBERS STUMBLE?

No one is perfect, of course, but too often people fail in building teams for the most basic of reasons:

(1) *Failure to paint the big picture*

For long-term success, people need to feel that they're part of something bigger than themselves. I have met few people, if any, who honestly enjoy being mere workers. Becoming part of the big picture and participating in the achievement of shared values is extremely important.

When the big picture is unclear, employees never see themselves as integral, indispensable parts of the team. Is it any wonder that such people fail or resign themselves to mediocrity?

(2) *Insufficient training*

People often fail, quite simply, because they are expected to do things for which they have never been prepared. Leaders tend to take resumes seriously, and team members often cover up inadequacies.

The education and training of each team member is one function that cannot be avoided or relegated to occasional group sessions. There is no substitute for one-on-one training. As a matter of fact, that is often the only way real learning can occur.

(3) *Telling, not asking*

The *telling* method implies control, indicates manipulation and triggers "bad blood" between authority figures and subordinates.

When an *asking* mindset permeates a company, it encourages creativity, inspires participation and reduces resistance to change.

Japanese managers traditionally have asked every worker to add ideas. And Japanese experts—for instance, engineers—live on the factory floor, supporting the workers.

American companies are learning. More than 900 companies, organizations and government agencies in the United States have structured programs for encouraging suggestions. During one year, those suggestions have saved their companies at least $2.2 billion. During the same year, visionary companies paid $160 million in awards for suggestions that were adopted. [4]

Oklahoma Natural Gas Company encourages employees to generate innovative ideas and methods that help the utility to be competitive, increase revenue and reduce the cost of service. Employees are encouraged to submit as many ideas as possible. The ideas are evaluated by a number of experts, and a committee determines which category the accepted ideas fall into: generating or saving up to $3,000, and generating or saving more than $3,000. The categories determine the monetary award for the employee. The person whose idea is judged Best Idea of the Year receives an additional after-tax bonus of $1,100, presented at a service-award meeting. [5]

One of the greatest ways to overcome failure, in any organization, is to establish an orientation toward asking versus telling.

By asking effective questions, you help people buy in. You give them value. This continual practice of continually asking people what they want and what they need is one of the most effective mindsets for any company that desires to survive and succeed in the years to come.

(4) Dictatorial leaders

Ouch! This reason for failure is much more widespread than most leaders would like to admit. Dictators today, not unlike dictators of old, issue orders instead of seeking solutions, and give lip service to participatory management while modeling autocratic approaches.

As the boss, the dictator does have the right to demand or cajole subordinates through authoritarian and manipulative techniques, but as deposed rulers quickly learn, the people just might not follow.

(5) *Low motivation*

Low motivation is another problem that often leads to failure. Unfortunately, when energy and productivity are down, most managers will deal with it by attempting to motivate their people through slogans and rah-rah speeches rather than getting to such core issues as values, purpose, vision and alignment.

Motivational talks and programs can increase the energy level and short-term success, but unless some substance is involved, motivational methods become little more than candy bar-type panaceas. When the sugar hits the system, it may increase the energy level for a short while, but the energy level will quickly plummet as the sugar burns out.

I believe in motivation, properly used. Increasing the energy level of a company is useful. The question is this: What are you motivating people toward? That question often goes unanswered in the dizzying excitement of typical motivational-type gimmicks.

(6) *Alienation*

The modern concept of estrangement is used typically to indicate non-involvement and an inability to develop firm commitments on the part of individuals within an organization.

This results in feelings of separateness and apartness, which causes turbulence and distrust. In many cases, workers back away from any feelings about their jobs.

Alienation takes many forms: powerlessness, meaninglessness, lack of commitment to the team's values, isolation.

Worker alienation, allowed to go unchecked, can permeate any organization quickly.

(7) *Personal problems*

No one is immune to illnesses, divorce, disappointments, burdens and struggles. Everyone must face these challenges from time to time.

Leaders who do not recognize personal problems, and who are not willing sometimes to play the role of confidant, mentor and counselor, will see too many dropouts from their ranks.

Failures do not have to be fatal. Values-based leaders can work to overcome their own failures while seeking to help team members face their challenges. That is the essence of teamwork and leadership.

CLEARING AWAY NEGATIVES

To be candid, most organizations, and the individuals within them, have higher values than they reflect in their structures and practices. There are a couple of significantly simple reasons for this apparent contradiction: For starters, the organizational system itself tends to work against the highest values of the people within it. What's more, it takes constant diligence to ensure that an organization fosters the highest values of its people.

Here are several of the best antidotes to negative values.

(1) *Common sense*

Make sure the right person is in the right position. People whose skills and training do not fit the job will waste valuable time and effort trying to do things they are not prepared to do.

Also, help team-members get a clear idea of what is expected of them. Low expectations and job overlapping will bring mediocrity and duplication of effort.

(2) *Openness*

Leaders should keep open-door policies when possible. Manage by walking around. Ask questions. Answer questions honestly. Be a real person, not an ivory icon.

(3) *Perspective*

Help people get to the heart of a matter. Too many people fail because they get so wrapped up in busy work that they lose sight of what really needs to be accomplished.

Make sure that all team members know what the big picture is, both good and bad, and what they will need to do to accomplish the overall goals.

(4) *Forgiveness*

What does this have to do with the **real** business world? I have found that when leaders foster a forgiving spirit throughout the organization, many of the picayune problems no longer have meaning.

"He who cannot forgive others," wrote philosopher George Herbert, "breaks the bridge over which he must pass himself."

Remember Benjamin Franklin's words: "Doing an injury puts you below your enemy; revenging one makes you but even with him; forgiving it sets you above him."

One of the best ways to create a climate of strength and synergy is to forgive. When people fail us, especially when we perceive it as deliberate, we don't need to ignore it. A true leader will help the person to acknowledge failure and overcome it.

Values-based leaders are forgiving leaders, regardless of the outcome.

OPENINGS

Clearing away negative values and hindrances can mean the beginning of something wonderful and life-changing. Let me illustrate:

Laurens Van der Post, an African writer of *The Seed and the Sower* begins his book with a true story. He opens the chapter with the words, "I had a brother once, and I betrayed him."

The account centers on two brothers from a small South African village. The elder brother was handsome, tall, intelligent, a good student, a remarkable athlete and a natural leader. He went away to a private school and quickly made a name for himself. He was in his final year at the academy when his younger brother enrolled there to begin his studies.

The younger brother was neither good-looking nor athletic; he was a hunchback. Since he had been a small child, his mother had skillfully sewn pads into his jackets to conceal his spinal deformity. He was so sensitive about his short, curved stature that nobody in the family ever spoke openly of it. Yet the boy had one great gift: He could sing gloriously. Everyone was amazed at his exceptional talent.

As was the custom in the academy, soon after the younger brother's arrival, the older students held an initiation, which consisted of a public humiliation of each new pupil, supposedly to extract proof of courage.

Each year one student was singled out to be the scapegoat, and was mercilessly hounded. The younger brother was that person, and during the evening of initiation, the students carried him to the water tower. They required him to sing under much duress. When he sang beautifully, despite his understandable fear, the others became even more abusive. Finally they tore off his jacket and shirt.

Suddenly his never-before-seen hunched back was revealed for all to see. That brought even more catcalls and physical abuse.

The older brother knew what was happening, but he busied himself with work in the laboratory. A word from him would have stopped the tragic scene. As a leader, he could have acknowledged the boy as his younger brother, but instead he ignored the situation as the mob raged outside.

The younger brother survived the physical and emotional torment that night, but his spirit was crushed. He withdrew into himself and refused to sing. At the end of the term, he went home to the family farm and lived a lonely, reclusive life.

The older brother rose to prominence during World War II. He became an officer, stationed in Palestine. One night, while recovering from an injury, he lay under the stars and in a dream saw Jesus with His disciples. He saw his own face and body in place of Judas.

"I am Judas!" he exclaimed in the dream. "I had a brother once, and I betrayed him."

"Go to your brother," Christ replied.

When he awoke from the vivid dream, the man resolved to go back to his home as soon as possible. The long journey from Palestine to South Africa was incredibly difficult and painful. When he finally arrived, unannounced at night, he found his younger brother beside a fire, tending the irrigation for plants in the family's parched, drought-stricken garden.

The elder brother looked into the younger's dark eyes, seeing deeply how imprisoned he was in the past. The moment of betrayal was visible in the younger man's face, as well as in his twisted form.

"I've come from far away just to see and talk to you," the older of the two began. In a torrent of wrenching words, he admitted his tragic wrongdoing. Then he asked for forgiveness.

When he finished, the brothers embraced. Together they knelt in the field, arms around each other, a deluge of tears streaming down their faces and prayed for God's forgiveness to touch them both.

The first rainstorm of the year began during those moments, so both decided to run for cover in the house. The younger sent his brother ahead, however, since the irrigation water needed to be shut off.

As the older brother approached the family house, he heard music coming from the garden.

Though the younger brother had not sung since that fateful night, his beautiful voice rose over the sound of rain. The older brother recognized it as a song his brother had written and sung many times as a child. Then a new verse was added:

> *I rode all through the night*
> > *to the fire in the distance burning.*
> *And beside the fire found*
> > *he who had waited for so long.*

For both men it was a new beginning. The elder brother rejoined the war effort and later became a successful statesman. The younger brother rediscovered his rich talent and eventually rose to great fame in his country.

Why? They acknowledged a tragic mistake. They forgave. They started again.

Clearing away negative values definitely has a place in the rough-and-tumble marketplace.

VALUES SELF-CHECK

In your notebook, write short answers to the following questions, using these inquiries to uncover more about yourself and your values. Don't worry if your answers are incomplete:

(1) What are the three most gratifying or meaningful experiences you have encountered in corporate life?

(2) Right now, what are your three central goals for your personal life?

(3) How are those three goals different from your goals five years ago?

(4) What are the major obstacles to reaching your current goals?

(5) How would your life change if you did reach all three current goals?

(6) What would you like to stop doing?

(7) What is the largest change or crisis that you expect to face during the next five years?

The purpose of this exercise is to define areas and dimensions of your life that may need a fresh perspective.

VALUES SUMMARY

Anita was born in the Philippines. Her father never married her mother, and abandoned mother and child at Anita's birth. In 1957, Anita, with a burning ambition and a desire to leave the poor environment of the Philippines, left for Mexico with $50 in her pocket. She lived there for three and a half years, working as a singer. From 1968 to 1975, she took a hotel and restaurant management course from Cornell University. She subsequently went into real-estate sales as a broker in El Paso, Texas.

Anita developed a hatred toward her father. She couldn't imagine how he could have abandoned his own infant child and the woman who had given her birth.

In 1985, her father was dying. He asked her to meet with him, and asked for her forgiveness. She finally agreed to forgive him. The act of forgiveness released her from all the tension and anguish that had built up over the years. With her hatred gone, she began to blossom in her personal and business life. Instead of drifting from one place to another, always working hard for a living, she focused her efforts and became one of El Paso's top real-estate brokers.

Anita will tell you that holding a grudge is like throwing someone a burning coal. The person to whom the coal is tossed can duck it and avoid harm. But the person who throws the coal will get blistered hands. Hatred consumes only the person who hates.

Anita's experience in forgiveness also opened her eyes to the value of relationships. She acquired an understanding of where anger originates. While her father was dying, he realized that one of his reasons for leaving Anita and her mother was that he feared taking on responsibility. Anita was grateful that in the process of forgiving her father, she opened up new possibilities for herself.

Getting past stifling systems and the tendency toward negative values requires an effort that only the best leaders and organizations seem willing to expend.

Perhaps you have observed how some people fail many times, yet are able to clear away negative values and move ahead with greater zest and vigor than ever before. How do they do it?

In the closing scene of Shakespeare's *The Tempest*, Prospero says of Alonzo: "Let us not burden our remembrances with a heaviness that's gone."

Vivien Larrimore gives this advice in **Keys**, her much-published poem:

> *I've shut the door on yesterday*
> *Its sorrow and mistakes:*
> *And now I throw the key away*
>   *to seek another room*
> *And furnish it with hopes and smiles*
> *And every springtime bloom.*
> *I've shut the door on yesterday*
> *And thrown the key away.*
> *Tomorrow holds no fears for me,*
> *Since I have found today."*

It's foolish to cling to unresolved problems and difficulties from the past and to bring the burdens and worries about the future into today's schedule.

To help clear away negative values, follow and foster a policy of self-examination. Discover what the problems really are. Then move on. Expect the best from people and generally you will not be disappointed.

Values to Remember

(1) Often, the biggest challenge in communicating a new or clarified value base is to clear away all the inherent negatives in an organization.

(2) The human mind, unbridled, tends to the negative. The organizational mindset, unchallenged and unled, also seems to point naturally toward the negative.

(3) Failure is every aspiring leader's nemesis. Whatever the reason for the failure, it is often easier to cover up past failures than to examine the reasons they happened.

(4) No one is perfect, but too often people fail in the marketplace for reasons that could be overcome.

(5) Constant diligence is needed to ensure that an organization fosters the highest values of its people.

"I think most of us are looking for a calling, not a job. Most of us, like the assembly-line worker, have jobs that are too small for our spirit. Jobs are not big enough for people." [6]

NORA WATSON

PART III

LEADERSHIP VISION

Chapter 8

HOW TO INSPIRE VALUES-BASED PERFORMANCE

Chapter 9

HOW TO NURTURE VALUES-BASED CUSTOMER SERVICE

Chapter 10

HOW TO STIMULATE VALUES-BASED QUALITY AWARENESS

Chapter 11

HOW TO FOSTER VALUES-BASED HUMAN-RESOURCE DEVELOPMENT

Chapter 12

HOW TO MAXIMIZE VALUES-BASED OPPORTUNITIES

EIGHT

How to Inspire Values-Based Performance

*Leaders have a significant role in creating the state
of mind that is the society. They can serve as symbols of
the moral unity of the society. They can express the
values that hold the society together. More importantly,
they can conceive and articulate goals that lift people out
of their petty preoccupations, carry them above the
conflicts that tear a society apart, and unite them in the
pursuit of objectives worthy of their best efforts.* [1]

JOHN W. GARDNER
American Industrialist

PERFORMANCE

The most productive and creative employees are those who see
the values and goals of their organization as the best vehicles for self-
fulfillment.

That ideal does not always exist.

Daniel Yankelovich is a specialist in probing changes in basic
values that motivate Americans. His Yankelovich Monitor, an annual index of value shifts, helps corporate leaders study the impact
of shifting values on the marketplace. He writes:

*If you look at changing American attitudes toward
work, you can catch a glimpse of what is a major factor
contributing to the decline. People who work at all levels of*

enterprise, and particularly younger middle-management people, are no longer motivated to work as hard and as effectively in the past.

In the late 1960s, almost half of all employed Americans looked to their work as a source of personal fulfillment. Now, that number has plunged to fewer than one in four. In the 1960s, a three-fifths majority, 58%, believed that "hard work always pays off." Now only 43% hold this belief. Only 13% of all working Americans find their work truly meaningful and more important to them than leisure-time pursuits. [2]

It used to be that fear, money and reliance on the traditional work ethic were sufficient incentives for any boss to get at least adequate performance out of his workers. Not today. Nor should we look back at the "good old days" as the right management method—far from it.

Instead, we have the opportunity today to create something new. I see the changing mentality as a great opportunity for leaders everywhere to change the old way of looking at performance.

DEADLY DISEASES

Years ago, Dr. W. Edwards Deming first began talking about the "Seven Deadly Diseases" of business, and Japanese companies were the first to listen. Eventually, after getting powdered in the marketplace, U.S. leaders began to understand what he was saying. The corporate illnesses he warned about are: [3]

(1) Lack of constancy or purpose.

(2) Emphasis on short-term profits.

(3) Evaluation by performance, merit rating or annual review of performance.

(4) Job-hopping management.

(5) Running a company on visible figures alone.

(6) Excessive medical costs.

(7) Excessive legal costs.

Dr. Deming insists that the effects of these factors are devastating—teamwork is destroyed; rivalry is nurtured. There is a better way, and it is up to today's leaders to find it.

CORE ISSUES

If fear, money and reliance on the traditional work ethic are no longer sufficient incentives for leaders to motivate their team members, what is?

Effective, long-term-oriented leaders know they must deal with the core causes of the performance issue. They must become fascinated with finding out everything they can about what inspires great performance on the job. The best answers cannot be "cookie-cutter" solutions, but must be different for every organization and team member.

Whatever process or system is used must merely be the catalyst—the approach that causes people to discover their potential, both as team members and as individuals.

I have found that an organization usually has a relatively small number of people who seem naturally to accept responsibility, give great performances and thrive on changes.

The great majority, on the other hand, see to accept responsibility only when forced, do the minimum that is required and resist all changes.

Ignoring this core issue is one of the most obvious reasons for low performance. Leaders make a mistake when they try to institute new systems solely for the natural peak performers, while ignoring the natural minimum performers, or vice-versa.

Leaders must deal with the entire team. More importantly, they must encourage top performers at the same time they are fostering ways to bring the majority up to maximum achievement.

Most notably, the less-effective majority consists of people who:

- Lack effective and appropriate focus
- Are taught what to think instead of how to think
- Waste energy on resisting change
- Are caught in a self-protective, defensive mode instead of in a creative process.

Somehow, the mentality of the lethargic majority must be turned around.

THE PRIMARY EMPHASIS

The secret to team motivation and performance is to offer something better, rather than taking something away. That means putting the emphasis on solutions, not problems.

The typical approach of too many managers is to concentrate on identifying and emphasizing all the problems in the organization. This can be just as counterproductive as ignoring the obstacles. When the focus is always on snags, there is no end to the problems that can be found. It becomes hard NOT to find something to fix.

Consider, for example, the ways an emphasis on problems differs from a solutions orientation:

THE ORGANIZATION THAT TENDS TO EMPHASIZE PROBLEMS:	THE ORGANIZATION THAT TRIES TO FOCUS ON SOLUTIONS:
* Spotlights what is not working— is wrong.	* Spotlights what is already working—what is right.
* Limits people's creativity.	* Tends to generate creativity.
* Creates defensiveness.	* Creates openness.
* Causes even more problems as attention is drawn to the problems that already exist.	* Is visionary in nature, since it spotlights that which is being built.
* Diffuses energy.	* Concentrates energy.

All that energy poured into finding and inspecting the problems in most companies becomes a millstone, holding the entire organization back from becoming great performers. That power could be practically limitless if focused toward identifying desired goals.

LEADERSHIP BY OBJECTIVE

What is goal-oriented leadership? Thus far, I have shared the roles and characteristics of leadership, but at its most basic level, it means the coordination and integration of all resources—both human and technical—to accomplish specific goals. The bottom line, then, is excellent performance.

Never forget that it is easier to manage right than it is to manage wrong—so much easier, because you create more time for yourself when doing things in an orderly, organized way.

Peter Drucker, then a well-known Harvard University economics professor, was the first to use the phrase Management by Objective (MBO). I prefer to call it Leadership By Objective (LBO).

For the values-based leader, LBO is a process whereby the team jointly establishes objectives over a specified time frame, then meets periodically—in team gatherings and one-on-one sessions with leaders—to evaluate progress in meeting those goals.

LBO, while not totally ignoring problems inherent in an organization, seeks to focus on results.

SETTING OBJECTIVES

Part of your role as a leader involves working with the team to plan ways to meet your goals, specifically in these 10 areas:

(1) Developing both short- and long-range goals and objectives.

(2) Sketching a plan of action or "work map" showing how the goals and objectives are to be accomplished.

(3) Determining the number and type of people needed to accomplish the team's goals.

(4) Establishing what is to be expected from each person.

(5) Probing the market and customer base (external and internal customers).

(6) Analyzing the work and time schedules that will be needed to meet or exceed the team's goals.

(7) Setting up training and education programs to maximize personnel capabilities.

(8) Developing support activities (clerical, technical & leadership).

(9) Giving input on financial aspects of the team's efforts.

(10) Assessing the types of reports made by all personnel.

While quotas and goals are never to be viewed as etched-in-stone prerogatives, it is vital to remember that anything that cannot be measured will never be prioritized. Measurable goals are necessary to establish your LBO program.

Why? Measurable goals provide regular feedback on results. These segmented targets increase motivation. More importantly, measurable goals contribute directly to the accomplishment of the overall plan of the company.

Therefore, make sure that all of your LBO goals have definite, written deadlines.

As a leader, once you and your team have agreed to objectives (in cooperation with other managers and executives), it becomes your task to translate those overall goals into tangible projections.

Visible, reachable objectives are critical to the success and direction of your company and team. Neglecting to establish projections is a sure route to failure.

It's up to you to be the translator of those goals, and this translation is the secret of successful LBO. You do no one a favor by trying to keep your team members in the "dark." If you want them to be part of your LBO effort, then you must treat them as vital, involved components in performance excellence.

LBO AND PERSONAL GOALS

Once company sales objectives are set, the focus must narrow to individual members of your team. Their goals should be documented in writing.

Since one of the most important tasks as a leader is to empower each person on your team—whether you have one, 10 or 1,000—let me suggest that you project a year in advance. Begin at the first of the calendar year, and breaking up the year into smaller units, perhaps months or quarters, depending upon your situation.

Here is one major key to LBO: Take the goals you set with each person, and monitor those projections in conjunction with actual performance. Be willing to make adjustments each quarter, based on your evaluation.

Why be so concerned, as a leader, with personal performance and goals?

I have learned the hard way always to set goals when working with people, regardless of their level of performance and whether they are veterans or new team members. A minimum set of projections helps all the people improve their attitudes, techniques, self-concept and time management. It helps them buy into the overall objectives.

INDIVIDUAL INVOLVEMENT

All team members should be given the chance to develop their objectives, goals and plans (subject, of course, to review and suggestions by leaders). With your guidance, each person should know personal potential better than anyone else and should be given the opportunity to help set individual performance standards.

This doesn't mean that the leader should not raise personal goals when they are set too low, but changes should not be made without an LBO discussion with the individual involved.

WHEN PERSONAL AGENDAS ARE REPRESSED

Alan, a good friend of mine, had a personal agenda in life. He worked for a company that allowed only one agenda: the corporate agenda. When Alan had to choose which agenda to follow, the company was the loser.

Alan had risen very rapidly in a large consulting group, and soon became manager of the West Coast division. The job called for 60 to 70 hours a week, including week-end work. The higher you rose in seniority, the more you had to travel. The job called for someone with a huge ego, and it offered a compensation package to match. Alan was earning more than a half-million dollars a year. But he was sacrificing time with his family.

After 16 years of working with this company, he decided it was time to start thinking about his family. Somehow, it seemed more important to be with his children at baseball games and swimming meets than to be consulting with Fortune 500 companies at all hours of the day and all days of the week. He didn't want to be a flashlight father—one who sees his children only by the light of a flashlight when he checks at bedtime to see that they're all right.

The CEO at Alan's company didn't allow personal agendas. He demanded a uniform standard, with no room for creativity. Alan liked to be in the forefront of knowledge, but he found no atmosphere for innovation. The company had lost its competitiveness; it was conceptually dormant.

Alan left it and became CEO of a small start-up company that allowed him a personal agenda. He invested his personal funds in the company. The company never succeeded though, and Alan lost several million dollars.

Alan felt strongly that he needed to work with people, giving strong service precedence over maximum profit. He wanted a company that would invest time and money in research and development to stay in the forefront of technology.

After his new company failed, his old company tempted him with even a greater offer as President of the company. Again he was offered a high six-figure salary. But he knew he would have to work long hours, traveling thousands of miles each year. He still had his personal values and his personal agenda. His priorities placed God first, family second and company third. He turned down the offer. The company's short-sighted rigidity deprived it of the services of an excellent executive.

LBO PERFORMANCE

Leading by Objective is an excellent opportunity for you to strengthen horizontal and vertical communication, since dialogue between you and your team is critical to performance excellence.

Your LBO approach should always emphasize results, not problems. Your motivation for building the team's performance objectives should be based on several factors that satisfy the human need for constructive accomplishment:

- Job content
- The degree of personal growth on the job.
- On-the-job achievement
- Recognition

You will find that with LBO, people actually begin supervising themselves. Their personal plans for reaching important deadlines are clearly defined. Self-responsibility, after all, is the key to everything that goes to *The Heart of Business*.

Team members, once they understand the LBO principle, enjoy knowing where they stand and where they are headed.

John H. Johnson, founder of Johnson Publishing Company (which publishes Ebony, Jet and Black World), Supreme Life Insurance Company and Fashion Fair Cosmetics, has said:

> *Success in business is a time-honored process involving hard work, risk-taking, money, a good product, maybe a little bit of luck, and most of all a burning commitment to succeed.* [4]

Simply put, the LBO approach builds that "burning commitment to succeed." It provides the opportunity to keep a spotlight on performance and growth for your company as well as for each individual. In addition, LBO clarifies future action.

But never forget that your LBO program will succeed only if the men and women who execute the team's overall plan believe they have contributed significantly in developing that plan. Ownership is crucial.

VALUES SUMMARY

Getting to the real issues of values-based performance means fighting the tendency toward easy, surface answers. It means resisting the pat solutions in the search for better ways to do things. In the marketplace, it means asking the simple-sounding questions about people, products and services. It means, in short, a total, sometimes painful dedication to truth.

M. Scott Peck, M.D., author of *The Road Less Traveled*, wrote:

> *Truth or reality is avoided when it is painful. We can revise our maps only when we have the discipline to over-*

come that pain. To have such discipline, we must be totally dedicated to truth. That is to say that we must always hold truth, as best we can determine it, to be more important, more vital to our self-interest, than our comfort. [5]

Granted, causes are often "soft" issues—important but not necessarily urgent. Most organizations tend to deal with the "hard" issues—highly urgent and seemingly important. Causes, therefore, largely go unnoticed until it is too late.

Values-based leadership and LBO can revolutionize a company's view concerning performance, especially in finding ways to spotlight objectives and results, not failures and problems.

Values to Remember

(1) The most productive and creative employees are those who see the values and goals of their organization as the best vehicles for self-fulfillment.

(2) It used to be that fear, money and reliance on the traditional work ethic were sufficient incentives for bosses to get at least adequate performance out of their workers. Not today.

(3) Effective, long-term-oriented leaders know they must deal with the core causes of the performance issue.

(4) Leaders must deal with the entire team. More importantly, leaders must encourage top performers at the same time they are fostering ways to bring the majority up to maximum achievement.

(5) The secret to team motivation and performance is to offer something better, rather than taking something away. That means putting the emphasis on solutions, not problems.

(6) Leadership by Objective (LBO), while not totally ignoring problems inherent in any organization, seeks to focus on results.

"People cannot be managed. Inventories can be managed, but people must be led."

H. ROSS PEROT
American Entrepreneur

NINE

How to Nurture Values-Based Customer Service

So long as we love, we serve; so long as we are loved by others, I would almost say that we are indispensable.

ROBERT LOUIS STEVENSON
Scottish author, poet and essayist

SERVICE PROBLEMS

Something is terribly wrong! Look around you at any area of the marketplace. How often do you see boredom, indifference and uncaring attitudes among those who serve the public.

This inattention to customers has become the most short-sighted, deadly and costly business deficiency today. Tom Peters, author of **Thriving on Chaos**, says it succinctly:

> *Sure, you can find marvelous exceptions such as Nordstrom's Clothing, Federal Express and The Limited, but service in America basically stinks!*

Customers are beginning to revolt. They are tired of being taken for granted, of being treated rudely and of having to accept slipshod service.

How ironic, especially since we now live in an increasingly service-based economy. These days, 75% of our work force is concerned with service in one form or another; yet complaints about service are at an all-time high. Servers in restaurants are frequently rude, mail often disappears, taxicab drivers are chronically inept and computers mangle our bills.

THE HEART OF BUSINESS

Why? For starters, statistically, our country faces an era of worker scarcity that may last into the year 2000. Even worse, more than half a million students in the rising generation drop out of high school every year, and 700,000 others who graduate each year are barely able to read their own diplomas.

What this all means is that people who want to work, who are willing to provide extra service and who are qualified will do extremely well in this environment. The doors of opportunity seem to be swinging wide open to people of both sexes who want to get ahead, whether they are older citizens or younger workers.

It's no surprise, given those statistics and trends, that the greatest shortages will be in the service industry. Of the 12.6 million new jobs created since the end of the 1982 recession, almost 85% have been in the service industry.

According to a report in USA Today:

> The problem is particularly acute in offices, where quality and productivity are extremely difficult to measure or improve. Errors are hard to pinpoint. Low-wage employ-ees are extremely difficult to motivate. [1]

That same article cites Martin Stankard, editor and publisher of *Productivity Views*, who insists that "Most offices actually could be run 300% better than they are now."

Service is no longer just a by-product of business; more and more it *is* the business. Realizing the revolt afoot among consumers, thousands of companies, from Wall Street brokerages to Illinois banks and California computer manufacturers, are seeking to improve quality and the way employees treat their customers.

No time has ever been so ripe for those values-based leaders to be come trend-setters in the area of excellence in customer service. In fact, those who develop this strategy can make themselves invaluable.

THE EXTRA MILE

This area of value-added service is clearly neglected and avoided? Why? Values-based service requires:

- Dedication to a spirit of service.
- Consistency of purpose.
- Going the extra mile as the norm.

When Nordstrom employees promise one-day tailoring, they are as good as their word. Domino's Pizza lives by its motto, "Delivery in 30 minutes or $3 off." Federal Express guarantees that it will "absolutely, positively" deliver overnight. Those guarantees force employees at all levels to go the extra mile, or the company loses its reputation.

All of us must consider ourselves salespeople and customer-service representatives, regardless of our job titles. All of us have customers (some internal and others external). We just have different names for them.

Many years ago, *Sales Management* magazine ran this superb article under the title, "The Name Means the Same:"

> *"The lawyer calls him a client.*
>
> *The doctor calls him a patient.*
>
> *The hotel calls him a guest.*
>
> *The editor calls him a subscriber.*
>
> *The broadcaster calls him a listener-viewer.*
>
> *The cooperative calls him a patron.*
>
> *The retailer calls him a shopper.*
>
> *The educator calls him a student.*
>
> *The manufacturer calls him a dealer.*
>
> *The politician calls him a constituent.*
>
> *The banker calls him a depositor-borrower.*
>
> *The minister calls him a parishioner."*

You may give a professional name to the person who buys your product or service, but no matter what you call him, he is always the customer.

No matter who you are or what you do, you and your team have "customers" whom you must serve better than your competition does.

No wonder Harvard Business School Professor Theodore Levitt has said, "There are no such things as service industries. There are only industries whose service components are greater or less than those of other industries. Everybody is in service."

Clearly, the businesses and individuals who succeed in the future will be those who recognize and adapt to the trend toward value-added customer service.

Values-based service will be the key factor not only in surviving, but also in prospering during the coming times of accelerated competition. In fact, value-added customer service will soon become the business of businesses.

VALUES-BASED SERVICE

Customer service. Everybody mouths platitudes about it, but how many companies and individuals are keenly aware of how critical customer service is to any business. From our experience as consultants and consumers, the truth should cause concern among all leaders.

Here is your challenge: In an age of carelessness and shoddy work, can you go the extra mile and do the things no one else seems willing to do?

Can you actually enjoy the discipline it takes to be an accelerated achiever?

A quick glance around you should prove that few individuals or companies are putting forth the kind of extra-mile effort required to provide value-added service. That knowledge, if you are willing to act on it, can add up to a virtual gold mine for you!

Values-based leaders must be concerned with customer service, not just because it is the "in" thing to do, but because it is the right thing to do. The person who decides to do whatever it takes to deliver value-added service becomes a member of a select group.

I belief that any company can effect a shift toward value-added, top-quality customer service. Here are the basic ways to begin:

(1) *Focus on your customers, whoever they may be.*

In a narcissistic era, this strategy seems rather outmoded. Actually, demonstrating total company commitment to quality customer service is one of the most vital principles of *The Heart of Business* for the future.

Don't just talk about customer service. Provide it. A quality service program will fail, but a quality service consciousness will succeed. The difference is enormous.

If you are a salesperson, for example, get beyond glad-handing and "How-ya-doing?" remarks, and into a client's real wants. Focus on your customer's needs, desires and problems.

(2) *Understand who your competitors are and then outserve them.*
This isn't as easy as it seems. You must understand your competition before you can expect to discover solutions.

Outserving the competition can be equally tricky. In financial services, insurance, and banking, for example, every institution is "selling" essentially the same services. This is when value-added service becomes *the* critical issue.

Writes Tom Peters in *Thriving on Chaos*:

> *Service pays! Customers for hamburgers, aircraft engines, fashion goods, bank loans, health care, and semiconductors buy far more than an interest rate or technical specifications. Over the long haul, relationships, based upon perceptions formed over time, are more important than so-called tangible traits.* [2]

Adds the best-selling author:

> *Every product and service can be completely redefined on the basis of "service/intangibles added." Service, on aver-age, is so bad that a barrage of tiny positives can overwhelm the competition. Remember, the average customer is neither a crook nor an idiot. Caution: Service is more than smiles—at the very best it's attitude and supporting systems.* [3]

(3) *Ask for continual feedback from your teammates and customers.*
No one, certainly not management, knows more about the needs and desires of a company's customers than front-line employees. Know your customer. Nothing in the world can replace sound knowledge of your customer.

(4) *Always be learning.*
The marketplace is constantly changing. Your workplace is unceasingly shifting. You must learn how to provide quality service to your customers not 75% or 80% of the time, but as close to 100% of the time as possible.

THE SECRET WAS IN THE CHOWDER AND THE SERVICE

I used to visit a restaurant near my office that was always full, because it served good soup, especially clam chowder. The service was friendly and very good.

I tasted my very first clam chowder at this restaurant. Subsequently I became hooked on it. It never tasted as good at other restaurants.

Eventually, the establishment was sold. The new owner wanted to increase profits. He was unable to reduce the rent and other fixed costs. So the first thing he cut was his variable expenses. In this case, it was his labor costs and his food costs.

In the case of the soup, he added water to extend it. He made a lot of short-term money. But the customers soon began to complain about poor service and the quality of the food.

I stopped patronizing the restaurant, and it eventually changed hands. The owner had changed the very things that had made the business successful.

The telephone company provides another lesson in customer service—or lack of it. Sometimes I drop a quarter into the slot of a pay telephone and nothing happens. Normally, I call the operator and ask her to call the number I want. I'm not going to go to the trouble of sending a self-addressed envelope so that I can get my quarter refunded a week later. I just want to make the phone call; that's why I put the quarter in the slot to start with.

A friend of mine put her quarter in one day, and the phone "ate it." She called the operator and was told that she could get her refund by sending a self-addressed envelope.

In her frustration, she kicked the telephone. Out poured 36 coins. She took the money and left, but her conscience bothered her. So she called the operator and told her what happened.

The operator told her she had to return the money to the telephone company.

"I'll be glad to," she told the operator, "if you'll send me 36 self-addressed envelopes."

When the telephone company—or any other business—ignores customer service, it is ignoring the very reason that it's in business.

(5) *Understand that you are in the PEOPLE BUSINESS, first and foremost.*

Whether you are a secretary, salesperson, share-cropper or surgeon, you must "sell" your products or services to people. The most difficult people to find are well-motivated, highly trained and concerned achievers who offer value-added service.

When you do provide "second mile" service, you stand out like a beautiful rose in the midst of winter. Think of your life during the past few weeks—how many times stand out as shining examples of royal customer-service treatment?

(6) *Be an invaluable consultant.*

Join your customer's team. Make yourself invaluable. Make it your mission to help solve the problems of your customer. Show a personal interest. This doesn't mean that you have to play the part of a phony psychologist, but you can develop a vibrant interest in the long-term needs of your customers.

Many people with whom you come in contact in your workplace niche—perhaps even a majority of them—seldom find that friendly, high-touch person in the high-tech, impersonal marketplace. By merely seeking to be a values-based consultant you quickly endure yourself to others.

One word of caution: don't fake interest. It shows. Truly become involved. The reward for showing interest can be mind-boggling.

(7) *Keep your word.*

Never break your promises, whatever the cost. One failure raises doubt; the next one raises tempers. More invites others to talk about you behind your back. Repeated failures will inevitably damage your reputation.

Make fewer promises and make only the promises that you absolutely, positively intend to fulfill.

(8) *Recognize your customers personally in meaningful, creative ways.*

Model this throughout your team. Use their names, of course. In addition, try recognizing customers (and this would certainly include your team members) personally in other ways and watch what happens. Send associates, clients and friends copies of newspaper clippings and articles you think they might enjoy.

I have learned much from a colleague who is especially good at sending personal congratulatory notes when he sees friends or clients featured in a newspaper business news section or in maga-

119

zine articles, or when that person's family members are recognized or honored.

This unique personal touch can include thank-you notes, birthday cards and thinking-of-you correspondence. Your thoughtfulness will pay off financially, and you will feel good doing something that others would never think of doing!

(9) *Empower your people.*
Writes Paul Hawken in *Growing a Business*:

> *The customer comes first? Not really. The employee comes first. Employees' attitudes toward customers reflect their treatment by their employers. They cannot serve unless served. There's no way to instill a positive customer-service ethic before you embody a positive employee ethic. Responsiveness in, responsiveness out.* [4]

(10) *Push decisions as close as possible to the customer.*

This should be obvious, but it is also very rare. Empowering your people means letting them make decisions. Employees in a renewing company become very good at making decisions, for they are aligned with a shared purpose and vision.

Without a strong, team-wide, values-based commitment to customer service, you quite probably will not survive the increasingly turbulent marketplace.

VALUES SELF-CHECK

In your notebook, write short answers to the following questions, using these inquiries to uncover more about yourself and your customer-service values.

(1) What is the primary purpose of your business?

(2) What are several guidelines your company already has in place to foster better customer service?

(3) How do executives in your company support managers and front-line people in becoming customer service heroes?

(4) For the people in your company, what are the major obstacles to becoming more customer oriented?

(5) How would your organization change if everyone, top-down, did become customer service champions?

The purpose of this exercise is to define areas and dimensions of your team that may need new direction.

VALUES SUMMARY

Ask, "What is the real purpose of our business?" The answer, no matter how you ask it, is customers.

You are a salesperson and customer service representative, no matter where you work in the marketplace. The better job you do in the people business, the greater your chances for accelerated success.

Certainly it takes motivation to be better, to respond faster and to provide a higher grade of service than others, but the workers and companies who do things differently are the ones who are just getting by.

Marketplace pressure has never been more intense, and it is just beginning to heat up. Customer service will make the difference in positioning you over your competition. Constant vigilance, supreme effort and true concern for your customer will win out any day over glitz and empty promises.

Values to Remember

(1) Value-added service is one of our generation's most widespread needs.

(2) You are in the customer-service business, no matter what your job description may be.

(3) Your challenge: Can you go the "extra mile" and do the things no one else seems willing to do?

"There is so much pressure to perform. You're under a microscope every time you move. But that's why we have the Olympic games. Pressure is what makes you better—if you just don't let it get to you."

CARL LEWIS
Olympic Track Champion

TEN

How to Stimulate
Values-Based
Quality Awareness

*The society which scorns excellence in plumbing
because it is a humble activity and tolerates shoddiness
in philosophy because it is an exalted activity will have
neither good plumbing nor good philosophy. Neither its
pipes nor its theories will hold water.* [1]

JOHN W. GARDNER

QUALITY

We have all had those poor quality experiences: the new car that
rattles, the motel room that isn't clean, the refrigerator that dies the
day after expiration of the warranty.

The plain truth is that this country has generally let quality slip,
and this problem goes far beyond the automobile, motel room and
refrigerator. Settling for second-best, it seems, has become a national
scourge.

That is sad, because when I grew up in Indonesia, America stood
for quality. Products made in the United States were coveted, for
they were almost always dependable and long-lasting.

Wealthy Indonesians drove big American cars and acquired
other American products as status symbols. Japanese cars and Japanese goods were looked upon as cheap—a notch above Indonesian
goods, perhaps, but far short of American standards. If you wanted
to be looked up to, you bought American, not Japanese.

My first American-made possession was a Parker fountain pen. I was in the sixth grade and the school had chosen me to participate in a city and county writing contest. I don't recall the subject of my essay, but I vividly remember choosing the Parker pen as my prize.

The second prize—a dictionary—would have been far more useful to me, and my teachers urged me to take it instead of the pen. But a Parker pen was the world's standard at the time. It was more expensive than the dictionary—and it was American-made. It was a symbol of my American dream.

What happened to this American reputation for quality?

Perhaps we lost it because the rest of the world was so intent on catching up that others passed us while we were sleeping. Maybe our slack attitude toward quality resulted from a mistrust of leaders, dating back to the 1960s and 1970s.

Writes Lee Iacocca:

> *Every day in America, 242 million people wake up, and if everyone would say when he gets up that he's going to do some classy, quality thing today that he didn't do yesterday, we'd be world beaters. Unfortunately, most people swing out of bed, yawn, and figure: "Oh, hell, I've got to make it through another day of drudgery." The attitude is that they're going to do what they're told and not one thing more. Now, how can you ever improve anything that way?* [2]

The auto executive added:

> *Quality, after all, is affected by something as basic as a person's sense of values. . . . If a person's going to do a good job, he's got to like coming to work. He's got to say to himself: "I'm going to help produce something great today," and he's got to say that every day.* [3]

The quality challenge is not a statistics issue. It is an attitude matter. It is a values problem.

More than half of all quality problems grow out of the failure of leaders to help their teams fully understand the company's purpose and vision. Workers who cannot see how their work fits within the total scope of the company's mission simply will not put forth the effort needed to maintain quality levels.

This lack of understanding makes it easier to fix blame than to seek solutions to quality problems. When hostility becomes strong enough, employees may even willfully sabotage quality efforts.

QUALITY AWARENESS

What is quality? Webster's gets right to the point: "The degree of excellence or superiority which a thing possesses."

Take 100,000 employees worldwide, $10 billion in annual revenue, declining market shares, a waning return on investment and a CEO who is determined to fight and win. That description belonged to Xerox in the early 1980s. Today, Xerox has risen to the top once again.

How?

CEO David Kearns and his team set their sights on quality. They began with a definition:

> *Xerox is a quality company. Quality is the basic business principle for Xerox. Quality means providing our external and internal customers with innovative products and services that fully satisfy their requirements. Quality improvement is the job of every Xerox employee.* [4]

According to Kenneth H. Hansen, Xerox's manager of corporate education and training, the concept of training for quality is not unique:

> *How we trained—our management process—is not unique. What makes it unique is that the training cascades from the top of the organization. That is, managers are trained first; with help from the training department, managers then conduct training for members of their family groups. One training principle guiding this effort is that no employee goes through training unless that employee's manager goes through it first.* [5]

As a result, Team Xerox has become an industry standard-bearer for top-down program development and implementation, visible and consistent leadership involvement and integration of the quality process into every element of the company's life.

It is a commitment that all values-based companies must follow to survive the coming years.

CORPORATE CURES

In Chapter 8, I mentioned the deadly corporate diseases recognized by Dr. Edward Deming, the genius who revolutionized the way most Japanese companies do business. Poor quality is inherent in each of those illnesses. Excellent quality must be present in each of the solutions. Deming suggests the following antidotes: [6]

(1) Develop constancy of purpose for improvement of product and service.

(2) Adapt the new philosophy in which negativism is unacceptable.

(3) Cease dependence on mass inspection.

(4) End the practice of awarding business on price tag alone.

(5) Constantly improve production and service.

(6) Institute continuing education and training.

(7) Instill leadership.

(8) Drive out fear.

(9) Break down barriers between staff areas.

(10) Eliminate slogans, exhortations and targets for the work force.

(11) Remove numerical quotas.

(12) Abolish barriers to workmanship pride.

(13) Activate a vigorous program of education and retraining.

(14) Take action to accomplish the quality transformation.

What do Deming's 14 points mean for U.S. companies? At present, most companies pay at least a fourth of their employees to correct the mistakes of the remaining three-fourths. I believe in forgiveness and a climate for experimentation, which sometimes allows for mistakes. At the same time, I am never tolerant of poor workmanship. Obviously, something must change.

Quality does not happen just because of end-of-the-line inspection; instead, quality awareness must be a beginning-to-end improvement of the entire process. The entire team must be committed to this improvement.

Quality is not a one-time endeavor. Quality awareness necessitates a progressive approach to look for ways to reduce waste and improve quality. Above all, employees should be taught *what* to think, not just *how* to think.

When I went into business, I started to research the ingredients of quality in a company. What are the common denominators of companies that embody the word "quality"?

At first glance, such companies seemed to have little in common. I found quality in high-tech and low-tech companies; in capital-intensive and labor-intensive companies, in old companies and new, in companies on the West Coast and companies on the East Coast.

I myself was involved in working for, managing and owning companies in fields as diverse as engineering, construction, fast food, real-estate development, brokerage and computers.

I finally found woven into this array of enterprises the common threads of quality. Here's what I found:

1. *Quality companies emphasize consumer service.* For a manufacturing company such as Motorola, the secret to success is simple: Just make the best product possible. But Motorola doesn't stop there. It has a policy that the customer is king; the customer is always right. When you return a product because you're dissatisfied with it, there's never a question asked. The company's strategy is to develop long-term relationships by giving what the customer wants instead of pursuing the quick profit. The quality company keeps its eyes on the consumer market at all times. It also watches production more closely than it watches the stock market.

2. *Quality companies emphasize the value of the employee.* In this company, the employees are involved in decisions that directly affect their jobs. They also share in the profits and ownership of the company. Training is emphasized to upgrade the skills of the work force. This training is not confined to technical skills; it also equips managers to play the roles of consultants to workers instead of work-place policemen.

3. *Quality companies emphasize long-term instead of short-term goals.* For example, Motorola used 10-year technology forecasts to predict and develop its five-year plans. Some of the oil companies are investing billions of dollars before they get any returns.

4. *Quality companies emphasize the involvement of leaders with the workers in the work place.* The days of executive suites, executive washrooms and executive lunchrooms and elevators are gone. Today's boss needs to know not only about finance but also about production and marketing.

5. *Quality companies provide a sense of ownership.* Managers are like the owners of small businesses. Their compensation rises when their contributions to the company rise.

6. *Quality companies emphasize job security for their employees.* There is an unwritten social contract with workers assuring them that they cannot be easily laid off. If there is a downturn in the economy, their work hours might be reduced, but they will not be put out of work. Quality companies often provide many layers of stability for employees. When big fluctuations in worker hours are anticipated, these companies use part-time workers, contractors or reduced work weeks to absorb the slack.

7. *Quality companies consist of groups of small entrepreneurs.* An entrepreneurial company knows that two basic functions underlie all its activities: It makes things and it sells them. The best way to make something and then sell it is to provide employees with incentives to take pride in their work. If they are proud of what they do, the product will show it. It will sell, and it will be successful. By fostering pride in the production, selling and servicing of their products, many companies have become successful small- to medium-sized enterprises in America.

I've tried to instill all of these qualities in my companies. Their success speaks for itself. I've seen others successfully blend the ingredients of quality into their companies. One example was related to me by Dr. Patrick O'Hara, a close friend of mine who was a supporting engineer in the computer product division of Hewlett Packard.

In the highly competitive computer market of the early 1970s, HP created its PC3000 computer system and rushed it to market. It sold well because of the company's reputation for quality. Within a few months, however, customers began to express great dissatisfaction with it. The technical staff was unable to solve the problems. David Packard, who was in charge of sales, decided that customers could return their products and get their money back. This involved millions of dollars, but he was willing to spend the money to safeguard Hewlett Packard's reputation.

Bill Hewlett, the technical arm of HP, re-evaluated the product and declared that it would be enhanced. He instituted a six-month crash program to bring the product up to quality standards and reintroduce it to the computer market. Customers who had bought the original product could exchange it for the corrected model if they chose. Otherwise, their money would be refunded. They would also be reimbursed for any expenses they might have incurred, such as the development costs of software applications.

The HP 3000 was reintroduced and most customers accepted HP's offer to replace their old models with the new one. The product became a very successful product line.

When the problem was first discovered, the morale of the computer product division plummeted. When it became clear that the problems would be corrected and that HP was going to stand by its commitment to back its products, the morale soared. Employees worked very hard to rectify the problem. They were all proud of the result and proud to be members of the company and the team that produced the results. That was more than enough reward for them.

IBM also takes quality seriously. One of its ads poses the question: "If your failure rate is one in a million, what do you tell that one customer?" The ad makes the point: "At IBM we treat every customer as if he or she is the one in a million."

The attitude of quality-first and customer-first must be woven throughout the process if it is to be effective. The roll-call of companies that have cultivated that attitude reads like a chronicle of American success stories. It includes McDonald's, Disney, Domino's Pizza and many other companies whose names have become household words.

You may have done your homework and developed a high-quality product that the public is clamoring for. But if you don't back it up with a quality customer relationship, you might as well throw out the order book.

Leadership, especially values-based leadership, consists of helping people become better people. Better people do a better job. Period.

When values permeate a company, quality can never be far behind. Team members must work together to solve problems, not create problems for each other. Open communication between areas must be established and encouraged. Only highly committed team members with across-the-board leaders will be able to carry out the quality mission.

Making money is not the bottom line in a business enterprise. The true bottom line is staying in business and providing jobs through innovation, research, constant improvement and maintenance. That all boils down to one word: quality.

Obviously, visionary managers cannot hope to achieve these guidelines without a broad base of team support. Likewise, aspiring team members cannot make such drastic changes without a leadership commitment. A critical mass of people in the company must understand how important the widespread awareness of quality really is.

Lee Iacocca says:

> *In Japan the commitment to quality is so ingrained it's almost like personal hygiene. And that's got to be our commitment too: to make that goal so much a part of our thinking that we don't have to think about it anymore."* [7]

To paraphrase the Ford Motor Company advertisement, quality must be Job One for every organization that plans to survive and succeed during the coming years.

VALUES SUMMARY

A values-oriented organization creates a free flow of information and innovation, which is vital to maintaining quality. I call this quality awareness—which goes far beyond TQM—Total Quality Management. I have seen this level of awareness help many organizations transform themselves from poor to great through a new spirit of cooperation and a mutual search for better ways of improving quality.

Pat O'Hara's experience with Hewlett-Packard contrasted sharply with his experience at another high-tech company.

From 1975 through 1978, he was involved with a high-growth company that produced a product line called computer output microfilm systems. It supplied them to banking, government, and insurance organizations.

The system was highly complex. It was designed to be an indexing and retrieval system for legal documents. It was supposed to store an actual physical image of legal documents and be able to retrieve them within 45 seconds.

The system never worked properly because of poor quality control in producing the software that made the total system work. Every time the programmer would correct one problem, the correction would create more problems in other areas. The company Pat worked for would never agree to support the cost of correcting the original problem. Because of this, it was constantly in litigation with customers. The leadership was more interested in profit than in quality, and this profit-above-all attitude eventually led it into bankruptcy.

Jamie, another good friend of mine, told me how a company she worked for went into bankruptcy because it put its own convenience ahead of the interests of its customers.

She worked for one of the top three tax-preparing companies in the United states. Its people were customer-oriented. There was no problem with sales, service or client relations. The staff was giving top-quality service in a timely and speedy manner.

Then the company's top leaders decided to use main-frame computers to process the tax forms. In one day, the COBOL language was exchanged for a new language. Management promised customers a new level of service, using enhanced features that had not been available before.

Prudence should have suggested that the old system be kept around as a back-up for the old system. That would have required updating the old system to conform with new tax laws. Convenience won out. Management rushed the new system into service and pushed the old system out the door.

By the time the tax season started, the computer was producing error after error. Jamie, who had enjoyed a great relationship with her clients, was dismayed to learn that program input and output could not be traced with the new system. She was flooded with complaints about erroneous tax returns, and she could do nothing about them.

Management had put all its eggs in one basket by using a system that had not been thoroughly tested, and had not been proved in actual operation. The result was chaos—and bankruptcy for a company that had once been a leader in its field.

The bottom line: the level of quality in an organization tends to be a reflection of the level of quality modeled by leadership. When management begins showing a true desire for quality throughout the organization, it's amazing how quickly employees buy into the vision.

"Walking the talk" must be consistent, especially in relation to the way leaders preach quality and the manner in which they treat employees.

Values to Remember

(1) The plain truth is that this country has generally let quality slip, and this problem goes far beyond the automobile, motel room and refrigerator. Settling for second-best, it seems, has become the national sport.

(2) The quality challenge is not a statistics issue. It is an attitude matter. It is a values problem.

(3) What is quality? Webster's says it is "the degree of excellence or superiority which a thing possesses."

(4) A critical mass of people in the company must understand how important the widespread awareness of quality really is.

Guido the plumber and Michelangelo obtained their marble from the same quarry, but what each saw in the marble made the difference between a nobleman's sink and a brilliant sculpture. [8]

BOB KALL

ELEVEN

How to Foster Values-Based Human Resource Development

The biggest tragedy in America is not the great waste of natural resources, though this is tragic. The biggest tragedy is the waste of human resources.

OLIVER WENDELL HOLMES
American Writer and Physician

WASTE

In a probing look at the decline of America's work force, **Business Week** began its analysis with this sobering statement:

The nation's ability to compete is threatened by inadequate investment in our most important resource: people. Put simply, too many workers lack the skills to perform more demanding jobs. And as the economy comes to depend more and more on women and minorities, we face a massive job of education and training— starting before kindergarten. Can we afford it? We have no choice. [1]

Bruce Nussbaum, writer of the lead article in the magazine's special report, added:

Who will do America's work as the demand for skilled labor outstrips a dwindling supply? The U.S. has lost much ground to competitors, and investing in people looks like the way to retake it. After years of neglect, the problem of human capital has become a crisis. [2]

The United States is still the dominant world power, but the economic giant now is constantly looking over its shoulder at Japan, Europe and other rising competitors. We have been far outdistanced in the race for a better-educated work force; in connection with that, manufacturing superiority already rests with the Japanese.

The yearly $150 billion trade deficit, combined with a foreign debt of half a trillion dollars, continues to reflect the inability of a large percentage of the American work force to compete as well as it must to survive an increasingly globalized economy.

Japan's functional literacy rate is nearing 100%, for example, while literacy in America has dropped to 80%. But illiteracy is only a symptom of much larger problems burdening our economy.

Says Merry I. White, professor of comparative sociology at Boston University:

> *Much of the success of Japan stems from the fact that its blue-collar workers can interpret advanced mathematics, read complex engineering blueprints, and perform sophisticated tasks on the factory floor far better than blue-collars in the U.S.* [3]

During the past 30 years, America has tried to solve these problems by pouring hundreds of billions of dollars into capital equipment and educational/social programs, but the country is discovering that it has been short-sighted when it comes to empowering the work force. Building up human capital must become a national priority. These problems will not go away, nor will indiscriminate spending help matters. The governments (federal, state and local), business, labor and education will all have to do their parts.

LEADERSHIP AT ALL LEVELS

What should be done?

- *On the most basic level, the education of our young children should be a top priority throughout the nation—corporately and privately.*

Teachers should be paid salaries comparable to those they could earn in industry, and the entire teaching process should be transformed into more of a values-based, teamwork-oriented, thinking-motivated process.

• **Businesses must foster an education-friendly environment.**

This should extend far beyond corporate day care. In fact, the most visionary business leaders have begun putting together resources, energy and influence to improve education. Hundreds of partnerships are blooming between schools and businesses. They run the gamut: gifts of equipment, paid work-study programs, teacher training, and literacy volunteers.

This is not a totally new concept. As early as the 1950s, the Singer Company put its sewing machines in most high-school home-economics classrooms. Campbell Soup was another pacesetter; for years schools gathered soup-can labels to obtain credit toward sports equipment.

Today's business leaders, however, are going far beyond those excellent pioneers.

The quality of every company's service depends on its modern organizational, training and educational capabilities. In our company, we stress training for all of our people. Not only do we train people in technical tasks; we also train supervisors and middle managers for their roles as consultants to the workers, not as police officers. That is one of the most important aspects of training we can emphasize.

We also need to emphasize that training does not replace education. It isn't enough to teach people *what* to do. We must also teach them *why*.

IBM provides an outstanding example of a company with a surpassing commitment to training and education. IBM may devote more time to the classroom than many universities. Every IBM manager, for example, receives 40 hours of training, and that commitment to training continues through all levels of the organization.

IBM invites its customers to participate in a variety of classroom programs. In our company, we also invite customers to tell us what we do wrong and how we should improve. We invite them to participate in our discussions and our training and educational sessions.

In fact, I believe that in any industry in which repeat business is essential for long-term growth, it is very important to make sure that the first order is only a starting point. The initial order is the beginning of a long relationship. Outstanding service is what really brings the customer back to do more business. That must be emphasized in our training and education.

In one of the most heartwarming, publicized examples of what one individual can do, during 1981, a New York industrialist named Eugene Lang challenged a Harlem sixth- grade class to stay in school. He then offered college scholarships to all pupils in the classroom who accepted his challenge. He paid for remedial and counseling staff and became personally involved with the young people. Of the 54 original pupils who remained in New York, 50 finished high school and 34 have completed all or most of the requirements for their college degrees.

In Dallas, more than 1,000 businesses have adopted the city's 200 public schools. The sponsors provide volunteer tutors, funds and equipment.

North Carolina-based Lowe's Foods Stores are cooperating with Silicon Valley-based Apple Corporation to put computers into classrooms. Parents are able to redeem grocery-store receipts to gain credit toward equipment.

This pattern continues in New York City, Seattle, Los Angeles and many other places. Business is ultimately the benefactor of educational excellence, and business will also pay for the downside of education's failures (through re-education, lower productivity and added taxes to support the men and women who are unprepared or unwilling to be productive members of society). It is no wonder that a growing number of visionary corporate leaders are beginning to focus on the importance of the vital role business must play in educational and leadership consciousness.

- *Businesses must also adopt major new incentives to train and retrain team members.*

In a competitive and rapidly changing economy, old skills become outdated and new skills are needed. It has been estimated that most people working today will change occupations three times and jobs at least a half-dozen times.

Elected officials could help spur a heightened interest in continuing education and training through tax breaks and laws encouraging corporate sponsorships or partnerships in the instruction of employees.

• *Businesses must realize that the work force is constantly changing and should make flexibility a key component.*

Writes Karen Pennar in **Business Week**:

> To retain female workers who have many years' experience, and to enable those workers to be more productive, companies should extend child-care benefits to a far greater extent than they have to date. To keep older workers productive, employers should offer new duties and more flexible hours. And granting workers flexible benefits could make them more mobile, and thus more responsive to the fast-changing labor demands of employers.[4]

Pennar adds this moving summary:

> Too frequently, managers have looked at workers as a cost rather than a resource. And every extra dollar spent on workers was viewed as that much more of a burden, whereas it could be, if wisely spent, a means to empower workers to do better. Hundreds of companies now recognize this to be true with respect to training. [5]

• *Leadership must become a national passion.*

Leadership training used to be rare. Today, more companies are starting to realize the need for leadership training and are providing it. Most companies, however, currently provide this training for key personnel only.

As mentioned in previous chapters, the emerging leadership-by-values role is part of a new pattern of across-the-board leadership that is becoming more and more common. This type of organization is leaner and flatter and more participatory, and has more of an emphasis on self-responsibility than traditional companies. This kind of values-based company is also characterized by greater cooperation between departments or divisions.

Increasingly, the original organization is being divided into "business units" that contain all the functions needed to run the operation. Currently, among my companies and with many of my clients, both production and support areas are being designed this way. It is a dramatic conceptual shift that is proving to be highly profitable and rewarding.

The first restaurant I opened is a good example of this. We thought all of us had a very good feel for management. I hired a manager to do our training who had previously been involved with a large chain of hotels and motels. He knew customer-service training.

Therefore, we were surprised when we surveyed our employees about the management team and were given very low marks.

At that time, I admitted it was my fault, because I was functioning as an absentee owner. Somehow, in the rush of running many businesses, I was not giving that restaurant the attention it needed. After all, I reasoned, I had given it a top-notch management team. Some of our managers had experience in the service industry and extensive background as trainers. A few weeks before we opened new restaurants, they spent a lot of time training, including classroom sessions, role-playing and dry runs. We also invited local business people to sample the food free. We tried to make the employees feel more appreciated than they had felt at other places of employment. We gave them free meals and drinks.

At first, the restaurant zoomed. The local business journal called it one of the up-and-coming restaurants. Although we had only 60 seats, we had daily receipts of more than $5,000.

But as time went by, our management began concentrating on opening other establishments. As we became engrossed in the task of finding sites and monitoring construction, we devoted less interest and attention to our original restaurant operation.

My managers readily admitted that we were looking too far into the future without looking inside. As a result, my managers and I were not there when we were needed, and the original establishment deteriorated.

Once we realized the problem, we made a complete turnaround in sales and service. We once again achieved great quality.

Another problem we experienced was the high cost of labor for food and service. We started to chop down on the service, and soon realized that this was a cardinal sin. When we lost our quality, the customers became dissatisfied. We were guilty of sacrificing the future by trying to make big profits in the present. When we rectified that error, we became successful. In fact, I sold that first restaurant for a very good profit.

It should be apparent to anyone with an eye on the future that skills in leadership by values are needed by *everyone* within an organization. If the company is to be quality-oriented (it won't survive otherwise), everyone must buy into personal and corporate leadership.

VALUES-ORIENTED LEADERSHIP ROLES

Lachlan McLean, an Australian manufacturer, has said, "You can only lead others where you yourself are willing to go." [6]

To empower their people, good leaders must be both well-educated and values-based enough to be willing to function in many different roles. Through the years, I have seen at least seven leadership roles: *dynamo, peacemaker, figurehead, overseer, broadcaster, entrepreneur and resource distributor.*

People who aspire to be values-based leaders should study these 10 roles and the skills that each requires, and begin focusing on weaknesses they perceive in themselves. These roles are:

(1) *Dynamo*

The leadership role relates to the person in an organization who is ultimately responsible for producing results. This role includes components of inspiration, oversight, education, work assignments and evaluation. Charismatic power is a plus. This is the role most people refer to when they talk about leadership, but it is certainly not all that is required.

(2) *Peacemaker*

This role deals with relationships. The peacemaker-leader must be a statesperson, counselor, problem-solver, bridge-builder, crisis-handler and negotiator. The role calls for huge amounts of patience, wisdom and strength.

Though perhaps not as powerful a function as the charismatic leader part, the peacemaking role is probably one of the most important.

A perceptive peacemaker can foresee organizational problems, foil potential personnel difficulties, foster a support network and recognize marketplace conditions.

Being a good disturbance handler, on the surface, may seem like an unnecessary drain on a leader's time and energy, but "fighting fires" must be done at critical moments. An attentive ear, an organized system and decisive action can be a leader's most vital "fire extinguishers."

One note: if you spend too much of your time handling disturbances, you are undoubtedly need to be more organized. Delegate disturbance handling as close as possible to the problem—to front-line supervisors, if feasible.

Negotiating is pivotal to the leadership role. Life, it seems, is made of compromises. Corporate life is a hub of continuous negotiations. As a leader, you must handle personnel problems and mistakes. You will have to bargain with suppliers and employees, negotiate agreements and resolve labor disputes. You will often have to be a shock-absorber, agent, intermediary, broker and go-between.

(3) Figurehead

This role involves speeches, awards, recognition and other internal appearances.

Here is the paradox: Even though people in a company expect the figurehead-leader to be a great speechmaker and socializer, this is usually the area to which most fast-trackers give little time or effort.

The better internal figurehead role you can perform, the better you will be as a leader in imparting a feeling of warmth, style and stability within an organization.

Similar to the figurehead (internal) role, the external persona requires the vital task of speaking in behalf of your company to outsiders. It involves speeches, briefings, media interviews and other functions as a company representative.

Sure, organizations of any size have public relations experts and media representatives, but there are numerous occasions when the leader must become the spokesperson.

Superior communications skills are extremely desirable, since the role of spokesperson can be effective only when it is played by someone who is persuasive, articulate and always prepared with relevant statistics.

(4) *Overseer*

This role epitomizes MBWA (Management by Walking Around). As a leader, you must be an exceptional observer, reader, listener and scholar.

Information is power, and any leader who wants to succeed long-term must constantly be an aggressive information-seeker. That data should come from a wide range of sources. The higher you get in any organization, the more you will be surrounded by people who want to develop their own information "kingdoms." As a result, the data that you give and receive will be increasingly filtered unless you constantly monitor a wide range of signals.

One of the best ways to be a good overseer-leader is to spend as much time as possible with people throughout your organization. It is no secret that many of the most visionary leaders in the country, from Sam Walton (Wal-Mart) to Lee Iacocca (Chrysler), rub shoulders regularly with men and women who actually do the work in their companies—and who have less to lose than upper management by telling the truth.

(5) *Broadcaster*

A leader must decide what information and power must be given to whom. Values-based leaders who earnestly seek to empower their people seek to be communicators of the corporate dream.

An effective broadcaster-leader knows that information, however important, tends to get lost or clogged at certain bottlenecks within the organization. Therefore, the best leaders use a many-pronged attack to break down barriers: impromptu meetings, small briefing sessions, organized staff get-togethers, frequent news and information sheets, letters, memos, and bulletin boards. Also, more and more leaders are using videotapes or closed-circuit television broadcasts to share their company's mission, especially when the organization has more than one location.

Remember, information is power. Knowledge, properly used, lets employees know what is vital to you and to the organization.

THE HEART OF BUSINESS

When values-based leadership is emphasized from the top, your people will tend to become more values minded.

(6) *Entrepreneur*

This role is critical to keeping any organization invigorated and competitive. It involves profit-seeking, risk-taking and opportunity-watching.

Entrepreneur-leaders give life to a company as they seek trends, concepts and new sources of income. Without this spirit permeating an organization, stagnation results.

Needless to say, long-term success as an entrepreneur-leader largely depends upon good judgment, the ability to delegate and the knack for getting others to buy into the vision.

(7) *Resource distributor*

This powerful role can be the leader's greatest future-builder or career-destroyer, for it focuses on developing priorities, making budgets and setting values.

No matter what your leadership position involves, as you move up the ladder, you will increasingly be responsible for different types of resources. You must make clear-cut decisions about how to distribute them.

Financial budgets are one of the most important features of the leader's job. Numerous other kinds of resources have to be designated as well—personnel, time, materials and office space. To do this job well, you must be able to envision future trends and needs, not only of the company's overall mission, but of specific situations under your jurisdiction.

People who desire sustained leadership positions must become seasoned experts at allocation. Some of the brightest careers have been cut short or destroyed by lack of attention to this critical area.

Is it any wonder that leadership roles are so complex? There are no single, simple ways to proceed. To be effective, a leader needs to play many roles simultaneously.

Each role is important, of course, but too many leaders concentrate on one aspect to the detriment of the others.

VALUES SELF-CHECK

In your notebook, write short answers to the following questions, using these inquiries to uncover more about yourself and your team-development values.

(1) What is your company doing to foster empowerment among every level of team members?

(2) What are several guidelines your company uses to determine qualification for development programs?

(3) How do executives in your company model an overall belief in empowerment?

(4) In terms of educational and training, what are the most pressing needs?

(5) What are the major obstacles within your team to greater human-resource development?

The purpose of this exercise is to define areas and dimensions of your team which may need new direction.

VALUES SUMMARY

How much can you empower other people?—that is the greatest leadership question!

In the musical drama *The Man of La Mancha*, Don Quixote meets a street woman named Aldonza. The man of La Mancha stops, peers at her intently. He pronounces her his woman, whom he will hereafter call Dulcinea. The wench laughs at him, mocking him with the facts that she is hardly a gentleman's lady. Still, Don Quixote sees potential in her and desperately tries to help her see how wonderful she could be, calling her his lady repeatedly. She screams that she is nothing—only a charwoman and strumpet. She is Aldonza, not Dulcinea. She then runs from the stage. At the close of the play, Don Quixote lies dying. He feels he has failed. At the last moment, the lovely Dulcinea comes to him. She has finally accepted his words—his belief in her that she is a gentlewoman and lady.

Sometimes another person can work wonders in your life, or vice-versa. That principle, in toto, is the foundation for values-based human development.

A great leader must develop an overall obsession for values and empowerment, especially since a leader's responsibility extends beyond merely directing others and assigning tasks.

Great leaders develop a keen instinct for underlying structural causes of problems, rather than relying solely on "throwing more people and money" at problem symptoms.

They learn to recognize ways in which people can resist attempts to change their behavior. Conversely, leaders also deduce how to identify organizational "leverage points" which magnify small changes into pervasive system-wide improvement.

When leaders truly begin fostering values-based leadership—in themselves, throughout their organization, in their community, across the nation and encircling the globe—only then will we begin meeting the challenges of tomorrow.

Values to Remember

(1) During the past 30 years, America has tried to solve problems by pouring hundreds of billions of dollars into capital equipment and educational/social programs, but the country is discovering that it has been shortsighted when it comes to empowering the work force.

(2) Building up human capital must become a national priority.

(3) It should be apparent to anyone with an eye on the future that *leadership by values* skills are needed by *everyone* within an organization.

(4) To empower their people, good leaders must be both well-educated and values-based enough to be willing to function in many different roles.

If you want one year of prosperity,
grow grain.
If you want ten years of prosperity,
grow trees.
If you want one hundred years of prosperity,
grow people.

Ancient Chinese Proverb

TWELVE

How to Maximize Values-Based Opportunies

Most of us as individuals often act as though we think the future is something that happens to us, rather than as something we create every day. Many people explain their current activities in terms of where they have been rather than in terms of where they are going. Because it is over, the past is unmanageable. Because it has not happened, the future is manageable." [1]

HERBERT A. SHEPARD
American Educator

LEADERSHIP OPPORTUNITIES

Leadership, in its most basic form, is producing results, or as Lou Holtz, head football coach of the University of Notre Dame Fighting Irish, said "Leadership is getting a group of people to move in a direction toward a worthwhile goal." [2]

Values-based leadership involves a solid commitment to making the most of people and opportunities. Throughout *The Heart of Busi-ness*, I have offered a wide range of practical, proven guidelines for building the leadership values of you and others. In this final chapter, let me summarize by extending a dozen potent leadership skill-builders.

(1) *Lead by example.*

Be people conscious. Create a climate that will lead to worker satisfaction in your company or organization. Understand the men and women. Try to see things through their eyes.

(2) *Tell employees exactly what you expect from them.*

Specify the results you want accomplished in terms of measurable performance. Establish clear guidelines and priorities. Don't make people read your mind. Unless you communicate your goals and desires, you have no right to be upset when those objectives are not met satisfactorily.

When employees understand a company's purpose and vision, they invariably become aligned. The key to all effective motivation is desire, and the key to creating desire is to foster understanding.

(3) *Be a good listener.*

Listen your way to success. Every person is superior to you in some way, and you can do immeasurable good to workers' egos as you simultaneously learn from them.

Always remember that listening is at least 50% of leadership.

(4) *Have a two-way door.*

Encourage employees to come to your office, but you must also get out to where people work. Make these contacts as normal and frequent as possible, rather than giving the appearance of royalty mixing with commoners.

(5) *Be patient.*

Realize that bringing employees along in their jobs takes time. Empowerment sees the end result, not the momentary disappointments. When goals are not achieved, make sure that you communicate your wishes. Be specific with your instructions and suggestions. Even when you reprimand, weave encouragement into the conversation.

(6) *Give your employees not only problems to deal with, but also opportunities to grow.*

Empowerment comes through a positive, people-building environment. Like follows like. If you are willing to make and admit mistakes, you give space to an experimental, creative atmosphere. Encourage participation in decisions and actions of the job itself—let the employees determine work flow or add input to organizational plans.

Support the decisions of your team—don't just give lip service to participative management.

(7) *Keep your promises.*

Credibility creates trust. Trust builds strong organizations. Values-based leaders love and respect themselves enough to accept responsibility for their own lives, and they refuse to blame others for things that happen to them.

(8) *Be a problem preventer, not a problem solver.*

Don't be around to solve all the problems. Empower your team by discouraging dependency upon you. Great leaders are proactive rather than reactive, positive rather than negative, and they know that no matter how bad things seem, there are always options. Leading people means giving people the vision to see those options for themselves. Ask for specific solutions to problems and tasks. Above all, acknowledge that you can't solve all their problems; that you are not perfect, and that the company is not perfect.

(9) *Tell the truth.*

Too many contemporary leaders have already learned that the trouble with stretching the truth is that it is apt to snap back. Also, be realistic with work assignments—holding the proverbial carrot out of reach eventually leads to poorer and poorer performance.

(10) *Pass the pride along.*

Empower people. Recognize them. Show prompt appreciation for good ideas and good performance. Be specific. Tell the person or group what they did right and how that success makes you feel. When you praise, give honest praise—avoid conditional kudos.

(11) *Reward what you want more of.*

This goes far beyond passing the pride along. *You always get more of whatever you reward.* That is true in any area of relationships or human behavior.

An organization is getting whatever is being rewarded. If leaders are not pleased with results, they should at what is being rewarded.

Ford Motor Company leaders, for example, receive 40% to 65% of their bonuses based on contributions to quality, with just 20% based on contributions to profit.

What does your company *really* reward people for doing? What kind of formal incentives does the company give? What about informal rewards? For what contributions or attributes does the company recognize people? What results and behaviors are praised? To encourage teamwork, reward the team.

(12) *Foster intuition and creativity.*

Enlarge each job to provide innovative experiences.

Can people actually increase their powers of intuition? Absolutely! Set aside time regularly for quiet contemplation, and encourage your people to do the same. Pay more attention to mental images. Jot down ideas and thoughts, and watch to see if a pattern or focus emerges from random words and phrases.

Intuition—use it. Develop it. You are going to need it more and more as you move up the corporate ladder.

In the swirl of corporate boardroom jargon, the proverbial "bottom line" must be quality-oriented leadership by values. Any ideas about leadership are sadly lopsided without a constant emphasis on values and vision.

VISION

Great leadership demands the ability to create and communicate a vision that points the way for others. The power of such a vision stems directly from its use as a vehicle for elucidating an underlying, and often intangible, organization purpose.

A vision is a mental picture of the company's desired future. Corporate leaders must take the lead in creating this mental picture, and in communicating it to the minds and hearts of the people who work for the company. When the entire work force buys into the vision, this mental picture becomes a powerful magnet pulling the organization toward the future it desires.

Values-based organizations must be deeply purposeful. A workable, captivating vision serves as both a vehicle for people to discover an underlying purpose and a source of power with which they can align themselves.

In a word, business leaders are typified by an *extraordinary vision*. This is the burning question (and often the determining factor in leadership success): How well can you, as a leader, transmit your vision of teamwork to others?

SHARING YOUR VISION

Leaders should have visions of where they are going. Everyone involved—superiors, associates, and subordinates—should know that vision. A CEO's vision should be translated down to the janitor, but even if the vision is not translated well, all within the organization can know where they want to head.

During these turbulent days, a lot of people talk about being victims because there is no overall vision. That is a cop out. All leaders within a company must support the corporate vision (if there is one) and must also create visions for their respective departments.

When you create a vision for yourself and your people, you become a positive influence. Your behavior and determination become a model for others to buy into. That power is a great responsibility.

Robert Schuller, the well-known minister, has written:

Commit yourself to a cause worth living for. Get out of the grandstands and onto the playing fields. Move into the spotlight of creative and constructive involvement. It is the risk-running racer on the track, not the hotdog-eating grandstander who gets the attention, the applause, the encouragement and, finally, the prize. Because the chance-taker is in the spotlight, he attracts support and succeeds. And he wakes up one morning with the really big prize— self-confidence. Remember what has been said earlier— self-love is gained through adventure. Attach yourself to something bigger than yourself. In involvement you will acquire a sense of belonging. By a commitment to people, projects or causes, you will have an opportunity to assume responsibilities. Responsibility generates self-love, for responsibility fulfills the need to be needed.[3]

Values-based leaders inspire others through beliefs and vision. These extraordinary pacesetters spread this vision through high standards of excellence and performance. They also create a climate in which people's abilities emerge and develop naturally in the course of getting the job done. This ability to empower others goes far beyond management style and personality.

Without personal mastery and the ability to empower people, a leader must ultimately resort to force and intimidation in the attempt to have people fully utilize their abilities.

But in today's marketplace, leaders are not able to bully workers for long. Yesterday is gone. Tomorrow's leaders will have to form a cohesive, winning team or face marketplace jeopardy.

VALUES SUMMARY

At its most basic level, leadership means coordinating and integrating all resources—both human and technical—to accomplish specific results. It involves the systematic study of work, organization, effort and results, and may also include economic analysis and accounting.

More to the point, leadership means making work productive and helping people achieve. It means meeting the social impact and responsibilities of the larger environment outside the organization. It means balancing the demands of today and the demands of tomorrow.

Take the steps toward empowering yourself and others with values. These steps will make a major positive difference in every area of your life. Master the concepts in *The Heart of Business* as you master yourself.

Best wishes as you take those steps.

Values to Remember

(1) Leadership is getting a group of people to move in a direction toward a worthwhile goal.

(2) Values-based leadership involves a solid commitment to making the most of people and opportunities.

(3) Great leadership demands the ability to create and communicate a vision that points the way for others.

(4) When you create a vision for yourself and your people, you become a positive influence.

(5) Values-based leaders inspire others through beliefs and vision.

"My experience with people is that they generally do what you expect them to do! If you expect them to perform well, they will; conversely, if you expect them to perform poorly, they'll probably oblige. I believe that average employees who try their hardest to live up to your high expectations of them will do better than above-average people with low self-esteem. Motivate your people to draw on that untapped 90 percent of their ability, and their level of performance will soar!" [4]

MARY KAY ASH
Founder, Mary Kay Cosmetics

NOTES TO REMEMBER

_____

_____

_____

_____

_____

_____

_____

_____

_____

_____

_____

_____

_____

_____

_____

_____

_____

_____

_____

_____

_____

_____

_____

_____

_____

NOTES TO REMEMBER

NOTES TO REMEMBER

NOTES TO REMEMBER

Bibliography

Introduction

    1 .   Written by Jefferson in 1816, at the age of 73, in a letter to John Adams.

    2 .   In the interest of client confidentiality, some names or extraneous details of actual accounts shared in The Heart of Business have been changed. Thank-you to those people who made this book possible.

Chapter 1

    1.   Jo Ann Tooley and Amy Berstein, "Measures of Change," *U. S. News & World Report*, January 1, 1990, p. 66.

    2.   Sylvia Nasar, "It's Gloves-off Time," *U.S. News & World Report*, January 1, 1990, p. 40.

    3.   Alvin Toffler, *Future Shock* (New York: Random House, 1970), p. 12.

    4.   Ibid, pp. 15-17.

    5.   John Sculley, *Odyssey: Pepsi to Apple . . . A Journey of Adventure, Ideas and the Future* (New York: Harper & Row, 1987), p. 265.

    6.   Clarence B. Randall, *A Creed for Free Enterprise* (Boston: Little, Brown and Company, 1952), p. 16.

Chapter 2

    1 .   Jack Griffin, "It's OK, Son, Everybody Does It," *Chicago Sun-Times*.

    2 .   James M. Kouzes and Barry Z. Posner, *The Leadership Challenge* (San Francisco: Jossey-Bass Publishers, 1987), pp. 16-17.

    3 .   Kouzes and Posner, pp. 24-25.

    4 .   Ibid, p. 21.

    5 .   Kenneth Blanchard and Norman Vincent Peale, *The Power of Ethical Management* (New York: William Morrow, 1988) p. 42.

Chapter 3

    1 .   Dudley Lynch and Paul L. Kordis, *Strategy of the Dolphin* (New York: William Morrow, 1988), pp. 195-6.

    2 .   Robert H. Schuller, *Self-Love: The Dynamic Force of Success* (New York: Hawthorne Books, 1969), p. 127.

3. Ibid.

4. Web Bryant, "Dreaming of the Good Life," *USA Today*, April 4, 1989, p. D1.

5. Lee Iacocca with Sonny Kleinfield, *Talking Straight* (New York: Bantam Books, 1988), p. 239.

6. Ibid.

Chapter 4

1. Michael Maccoby, *The Leader* (New York:Bantam, 1986), p.44.

2. Abraham Zaleznik, "What Makes a Leader," *Success*, June 1989, p. 42.

3. Ibid, pp. 42-44.

Chapter 5

1. Joe D. Batten, *Tough-Minded Leadership* (American Management Association, 1989), p. 220.

2. Ibid, p. 203.

3. Brian Dumaine, "Business Secrets of Tommy Lasorda," *Fortune*, July 3, 1989, p. 131.

4. John Sculley, *Odyssey: Pepsi to Apple — A Journey of Adventure*, Ideas and the Future (New York: Harper & Row, 1987), p. 135.

5. Warren Bennis & Burt Nanus, Leaders: *The Strategies for Taking Charge* (New York: Harper & Row, 1985), pp. 107, 109.

6. Robert H. Schuller, *Discover Your Possibilities* (Irvine, CA: Harvest House, 1978), p. 115.

Chapter 6

1. James M. Kouzes and Barry Z. Posner, *The Leadership Challenge* (San Francisco: Jossey-Bass Publishers, 1987), p. 42.

2. John Naisbitt, *Megatrends: Ten New Directions Transforming Our Lives* (New York: Warner Books, 1982), p. 215.

3. Peter F. Drucker, "Leadership More Doing Than Dash," *The Wall Street Journal*, January 6, 1988, p. 3A.

4. John Naisbitt with Patricia Aburdene, *Megatrends 2000* (New York: Warner Books, 1990).

5. Suzy Parker, "I Beg Your Pardon," *USA Today*, August 22, 1988, p. B1.

6. Harold Geneen with Alvin Moscow, *Managing* (New York: Avon Books, 1984), p. 135.

7. Victor Kiam, *Going For It!* (New York: William Morrow and Company, 1986), pp. 156-7.

Chapter 7

1 . R. B. Reich, *The Next American Frontier* (New York: Times Books, 1983), p. 215.
2 . Carol Hymowitz, "Reasons Managers Fail," *The Wall Street Journal*, May 2, 1988, p. 1.
3 . Ibid, p. 2.
4 . Marcia Staimer, "Suggestion Box Pays Off," *USA Today*, March 15, 1989, p. 1B.
5 . "Ideas for Progress Plan," *Executive Communications*, Septem-ber 1988, p. 3.
6 . Studs Terkel, *Working* (New York: Pantheon Books, 1974), p. xxiv.

Chapter 8

1 . John W. Gardner, "The Antileadership Vaccine," Annual Report of the Carnegie Corporation, 1965, p. 12.

2 . Daniel Yankelovich, "Yankelovich on Today's Workers," *Industry Week*, December 18, 1979. p. 2.

3 . Mary Walton, *The Deming Management Method* (New York: Perigee Books, 1986), pp. 36-37.

4 . John H. Johnson, *Harvard Business Review*, March-April 1976, p. 124.

5 . M. Scott Peck, M.D., *The Road Less Traveled* (New York: Simon & Schuster, 1978), pp. 50-51.

Chapter 9

1 . John Hillkirk, "Service Problems," *USA Today*, August 14, 1988, p. 2A.

2 . Tom Peters, *Thriving on Chaos: Handbook for a Management Revolution* (New York: Harper & Row, 1987), p. 108.

3 . Ibid.

4 . Paul Hawken, *Growing a Business* (New York: Simon & Schuster, 1987), p. 197.

Chapter 10

1 . Roger von Oech, Ph.D., *A Whack on the Side of the Head* (New York: Warner Books, 1983), p. 18.

2 . Lee Iacocca with Sonny Kleinfield, *Talking Straight* (New York: Bantam Books, 1988),pp. 254-5.

3 . Ibid, p. 254.

4 . "Xerox Trains for Quality," *Management Development Report*, Summer 1988, p. 8.

5. Ibid.

6. Dr. Edward Deming's 14 points are adapted from Christopher E. Olstead, "Quality Management: The Deming Philosophy," *Control*, May 1989, pp. 70-73, and Mary Walton, *The Deming Management Method* (New York: Perigee Books, 1986), pp. 34-36.

7. Iacocca, p. 253.

8. Bob Kall, "Vision," *Reader's Digest*, August 1986, p. 78.

Chapter 11

1. "Human Capital: The Decline of America's Work Force," *Business Week*, September 19, 1989, cover.

2. Bruce Nussbaum, "Needed: Human Capital," *Business Week*, September 19, 1989, p. 100.

3. Ibid, p. 101.

4. Karen Pennar, "It's Time to Put Our Money Where Our Future Is," *Business Week*, September 19, 1989, p. 120.

5. Ibid, p. 121.

6. Lachlan McLean, quoted from James M. Kouzes and Barry Z. Posner, *The Leadership Challenge* (San Francisco: Jossey-Bass Publishers, 1987), p. 101.

Chapter 12

1. Peter Brill, M.D., and John P. Hayes, *Taming Your Turmoil* (Englewood Cliffs, NJ: Prentice-Hall, 1981), p. 69.

2. Gerhard Gschwandtner, "Three Sales Management Lessons from Coach Lou Holtz," *Personal Selling Power*, January/February 1989, p. 44.

3. Robert H. Schuller, Self-Love: *The Dynamic Force of Success* (New York: Hawthorn Books, 1969), p. 134.

4. Mary Kay Ash, *Mary Kay on People Management* (New York: Warner Books, 1984), p. 17.

The Author

Herman Suryoutomo, Ph.D., is a dynamic speaker, author, seminar leader. He is president and founder of a number of U.S. -based companies. He also serves as management/educational consultant to numerous firms.

A native of Indonesia, the author spent his formative years in extreme poverty. As a teenager, his childhood dream of coming to learn and work in the United States came true when he received the prestigious Fulbright Scholarship. After receiving advanced degrees in engineering and business administration from major universities in the USA, he built a career as owner, founder and CEO of companies in such diverse fields as engineering, real estate, computers and fast food restaurants.

He has been honored in *Who's Who in Industry and Finance, Who's Who in the World, Who's Who in the West, Who's Who in California* and *Men of Achievement,* and serves on boards of directors of several well-known charitable organizations in California and Nevada.

Now, Dr. Suryoutomo has written *The Heart of Business.* Some executives are already calling it the most readable, insightful and helpful book on the subject of corporate perspectives. His multi-dimensional, strategic approach to leadership values evolved from years of leading companies into marketplace success. He openly challenges cut-throat and stab-in-the-back mentalities.

Using more than three decades of successful experience, the author has created a dynamic set of proven, workable guidelines for developing long-term, across-the-board leadership in any organization.

Along his circuitous journey, the author has learned many simple guidelines for achievement in today's intensely complicated world. These principles are the foundations for *The Heart of Business.*

FILL IN AND MAIL . . . . TODAY

INNOVA PUBLISHING
P.O.BOX 3502
FREMONT, CA 94539

or order by phone or FAX
Phone **(510) 745-0200**   • FAX **(510)745-7124**
(Monday-Friday 9-5 PST)

Dear People at INNOVA Publishing,

I'd like to order copies of the following title:

Quantity	**Title**	**Amount**
_____	The Heart of Business	_____
	Sub-total	$_____
	Postage and Handling	2.00
	Sales Tax	$_____
	TOTAL (U.S. funds only)	$_____

( ) Check enclosed for $_____ (Payable to INNOVA)

Name _____

Address _____

City/State/Zip _____

Daytime telephone: _____

MONEY BACK GUARANTEE
(You must be satisfied or your money back)
Thank-you for your order

Southern
Hospitality